Mecca
THE BLESSED

Medina
THE RADIANT

The Holiest Cities of Islam

Photography by **Ali Kazuyoshi Nomachi**

Text by **Seyyed Hossein Nasr**

TUTTLE Publishing

Tokyo | Rutland, Vermont | Singapore

Published by Tuttle Publishing, an imprint of
Periplus Editions (HK) Ltd

A book project realized with the support of
Thaara International, Jeddah, Saudi Arabia

ISBN: 978-0-8048-4382-9 (English edition)
        978-0-8048-4383-6 (Bilingual edition)

Distributed by
North America, Europe & Middle East
Tuttle Publishing
364 Innovation Drive, North Clarendon,
VT 05759-9436 USA
Tel: 1 (802) 773-8930; Fax: 1 (802) 773-6993
info@tuttlepublishing.com / www.tuttlepublishing.com

Japan
Tuttle Publishing
Yaekari Building, 3rd Floor
5-4-12 Osaki, Shinagawa-ku, Tokyo 141-0032
Tel: (81) 3 5437-0171; Fax: (81) 3 5437-0755
sales@tuttle.co.jp / www.tuttle.co.jp

Asia Pacific
Berkeley Books Pte Ltd
61 Tai Seng Avenue, #02-12,
Singapore 534167
Tel: (65) 6280 1330; Fax: (65) 6280 6290
inquiries@periplus.com.sg / www.periplus.com

Indonesia
PT Java Books Indonesia
Kawasan Industri Pulogadung, Jl. Rawa Gelam IV
No. 9, Jakarta 13930
Tel: (61) 21 4682 1088; Fax: (61) 21 461 0206
crm@periplus.co.id / www.periplus.com

16 15 14 13   5 4 3 2 1
Printed in Singapore   1306TW

PAGE 1 The Ka'bah seen from the southeast,
the direction of Yemen.

PAGE 2 Prayers in the evening of Laylat-al Qadr.

CONTENTS

9   The Holiest Cities of Islam

47   Mecca the Blessed

74   Stages in the Hajj Pilgrimage

111   Medina the Radiant

169   The Arabian Peninsula

192   Glossary

PAGES 6–7 Pilgrims at Jabal Uhud, north of Medina, before dawn. It was here that on 23 March 625 (AH 3) the Islamic army led by the Blessed Prophet suffered a crushing defeat at the hands of the Meccan army in a major battle of the early history of Islam during which the Prophet himself was injured.

ABOVE *Tawaf* or circumambulation around the Ka'bah. *Tawaf* is a required part of the Hajj and must be performed seven times counter-clockwise starting at the southeastern corner of the Ka'bah where the Black Stone, symbol of the original covenant between God and man, is embedded.

In the Name of God, the Infinitely Good, the All-Merciful

The Holiest Cities of Islam

"And this is a Book which We have sent down full of blessings and confirming what [was revealed] before it: that thou mayest warn the Mother of Cities [Umm al-qura—Mecca] and its surroundings Those who believe in the hereafter believe herein and they are constant in their prayers."
—**Qur'an, vi: 92, trans. Yusuf Ali, modified**

"Medina is best for them if they only knew. No one leaves it through dislike of it without God putting in it someone better than he in place of him, and no one will remain there in spite of its hardship and distress without my being an intercessor on his behalf on the day of resurrection."
—**Saying (*hadith*) of the Prophet of Islam, in Muhammad ibn Abd Allah Khatib al-Tibrizi,**
***Mishkat al-Masabih*, trans. James Robson, Lahore: Muhammad Ashraf, 1981, pp. 586–7**

Two events, which in fact are two aspects of the same reality, cast the cities of Mecca (Makkah) and Medina (Madinah) in a short period upon the pages of world history. These events were the birth in AD 570, the maturity and prophethood of Muhammad ibn Abd Allah—peace and blessings be upon him—and the descent of the Qur'anic revelation upon him during a 23-year period from 610 until his death in 632. These events of cosmic proportions established Islam, the last plenary religion of humanity, upon the earth, thereby transforming not only the history of Arabia or of the Mediterranean basin and the Persian and Byzantine Empires, but also of lands as far away as France and the Philippines and, ultimately, the whole of the globe. The revelation of the Noble Qur'an, the verbatim Word of God for Muslims, began in Mecca where the Blessed Prophet was born and continued in Medina where he died. The very landscape of these two cities still reverberates with the grace (*barakah*) of the revelation and echoes the presence of that most perfect human being who was chosen by God to receive His last message and thereby to bring to completion the cycle of prophecy which had begun with Adam himself.

Mecca the Blessed (*al-Makkat al-mukarramah*) and Medina the Radiant (*al-Madinat al-munawwarah*), as they are known to Muslims, became intertwined by the very events of the Islamic revelation. Mecca, the city where the primordial Temple and House of God, the Ka'bah, is situated, was where the Prophet was born and raised while Medina became his city by virtue of his migration there in AD 622, which marks the beginning of the Islamic calendar. The very name Medina, which in Arabic means simply "city", is, in fact, the abbreviation of Madinat al-nabi, "the City of the Prophet", which replaced the older name of Yathrib after the Blessed Prophet migrated to that city where he established the first Islamic community and the first mosque.

The testimony whereby a person embraces Islam is simply "la ilaha illa'Llah" (there is no divinity but Allah) and "Muhammadun rasul Allah" (Muhammad is the messenger of God), "Allah" being simply the Arabic word for God considered in His absolute Oneness beyond all hypostatic differentiations. These two formulas are inseparable in Islamic life and are seen by Muslims as being inwardly united. One may say that such is also the case of Mecca and Medina, the two holy centers of Islam, whose significance is inseparable in the religious life and thought of Muslims. Mecca is primarily the city of God by virtue of the Kab'ah and may be said to correspond to "la ilaha illa'Llah", while Medina, where the Mosque of the Prophet and his tomb are to be found, is of course primarily the city of the Prophet and corresponds to "Muhammadun rasul Allah". And in the same way that five times a day the call to prayer (*al-adhan*), heard from minarets and rooftops as well as in streets and houses throughout the Islamic World, announces the two testimonies of faith together, the *barakah* and significance of those holy cities remain organically united. At the same time, their influence, and the second by virtue of the first, has over the centuries dominated not only the heartland of Islam in Arabia but all Islamic lands near and far, and love for them is cherished in the hearts of men and women of all different races and climes where there has been a positive response to the call to unity (*al-tawhid*) of the Islamic message.

Masjid al-Haram, the Grand Mosque of Mecca, a hundred years ago. In this photograph, the sacred spring Zamzam is located in a peak-roofed building adjacent to the Ka'bah. Today, the buildings in close proximity to the Ka'bah have been demolished and access to the spring of Zamzam has been moved underground.

The Arabian Peninsula

The peninsula of Arabia is located at the crossroad of three continents, Asia, Africa and Europe, its northern regions neighboring the Mediterranean world, its eastern realms Persia, and its southern shores Africa, with which it has always enjoyed close links in trade, migration of ideas and also people, as it has with its other neighbors. The southern region of the peninsula, home to ports through which goods were brought from the Indian Ocean, has always been more green than the north and was the home of many ancient civilizations. Its people, who considered themselves descendants of Qahtan, became known for the wonderful plants and perfumes that they cultivated. The frankincense and myrrh of southern Arabia were so well known in the Roman Empire that the Romans called this region Arabia Odorifera. It is sufficient to think of the Queen of Sheba and her world to recall the great regard that peoples of antiquity held for the high civilizations of southern Arabia.

As for the northern part of the peninsula, it was adjacent to the great Semitic civilizations of Mesopotamia, the influence of whose art is to be seen in the artifacts found in the north. Later, there were also close contacts with the Persian and Byzantine Empires. In the centuries between the rise of Christianity and the advent of Islam, there were, in fact, local kingdoms in the north such as the Nabataean and the Ghassanid which exercised influence upon certain aspects of the cultures of Arabia, the latter having been Christian.

Map of the center of Medina, dated 1790, when the city was surrounded by ramparts with the Mosque of the Prophet at its heart. The ramparts seen here, 2,300 meters long with four gates, were completed in 948/1541.

The heartland of Arabia, consisting of Hijaz and Najd, continued, however, to be dominated mostly by Arab nomads who had remained on the margin of the major historical developments to their north and were not greatly influenced by either Judaism or Christianity despite the presence of members of both communities in the cities of Arabia. As far as Hijaz, the sacred land in which Mecca and Medina are located, is concerned, it is the name of the western region of the Arabian peninsula, consisting of a fairly narrow tract of land about 1,400 kilometers long east of the Red Sea with the Tropic of Cancer running through its center. The land is called Hijaz, meaning "barrier", because its backbone, the Sarat Mountains, running parallel to the Red Sea, separates the flat coastal area called Tihamah from the highlands of Najd. The Sarat Mountains consist of volcanic peaks and natural depressions, creating a stark and rugged environment dominated by intense sunlight and with little rain. And it is in one of the natural depressions of this mountain range that is to be found the sacred city of Mecca, the hub of the earth and its center for the descendants of Ismail (the biblical Ishmael).

Arabia is dominated by deserts that before modern times could not be crossed except with the help of camels which, therefore, became indispensable to the life of its people. The population centers have always been situated around wells and springs in the desert which have created the oases for which certain desert areas are well known. The majority of the population of Arabia consisted of nomads, although cities such as Mecca existed in Arabia even before the rise of Islam. It was, however, only during the twentieth century that the vast majority of the nomads of Arabia became sedentarized and attempts were made to use the vast underground water sources of the peninsula to create agriculture for the settled nomads. Throughout history, the Arabs, the descendants of Ishmael (Ismail), were mostly nomads of Semitic stock. Something essential of the spiritual dimension of Semitic nomadism was, in fact, adopted by Islam and has therefore become a basic aspect of the spiritual universe of all Muslims.

Mecca's Early Sacred History

From the Islamic point of view, Mecca, the Ka'bah and the environs of the holy city are associated with the very origin of humanity and Islam's sacred history which, being based on the chain of prophecy, begins with Adam himself. The spiritual anthropology of Islam stated in the Qur'an begins with the creation of Adam and Eve in Paradise, their subsequent fall, which is not, however, associated with original sin in the Christian sense, and their search for each other on earth. Traditional sources mention that Adam descended in the island of Sarandib, or present-day Sri Lanka, and Eve in Arabia. Adam then set out to find Eve and finally encountered her at the plain of Arafat, so central to the rite of the annual pilgrimage to this day. Here, the two halves of primordial man, in the sense of *anthropos* and not only the male, became united again, and therefore it is here that one must search for the origin of the human family. It was also in this area in Mecca, then called Becca (Bakkah or "narrow valley"), that Adam built the first temple, the Ka'bah, as the earthly reflection of the Divine Throne and the prototype of all temples. Adam is said to have died and been buried in Mecca and Eve in Jeddah by the sea which still bears her name, Jiddah, meaning "maternal ancestor" in Arabic. The area of Mecca with the Ka'bah at its heart is therefore associated with primordiality, essential to Islam which considers itself as the reassertion of primordial monotheism and addresses what is primordial in the human soul, hence its also being called *din al-hanif* (the primordial religion) and *din al-fitrah* (the religion of one's primordial nature).

Nor are the main later stages of Islamic sacred history separated from the area of Mecca. According to tradition, when the flood occurred, the body of Adam, which had been interred in Mecca, began to float on the water while the ark of Noah circumambulated around it and the Ka'bah seven times before setting out north where it landed after the flood. A thousand years later, the great patriarch of monotheism, Abraham, or Ibrahim, came to Mecca with his Egyptian wife Hagar (Hajar) and their child Ishmael

Prayers in the evening of Laylat al-Qadr,
normally celebrated on the 27th day of Ramadan.

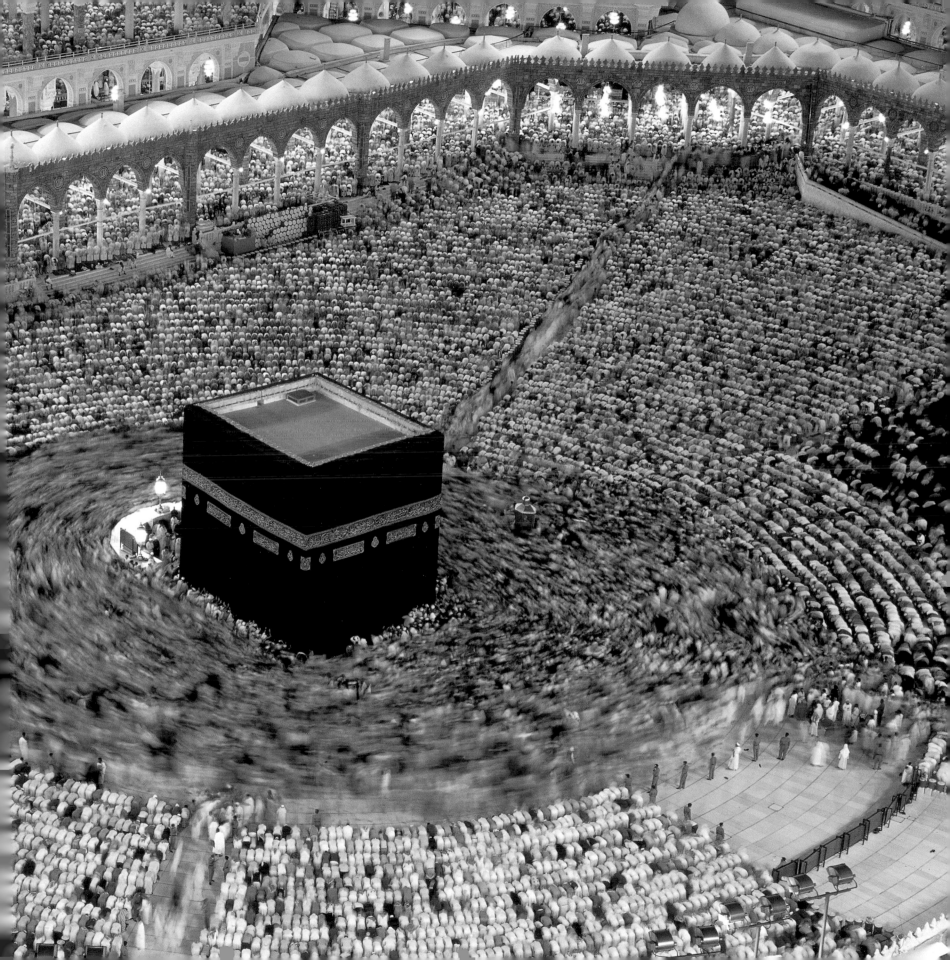

(Ismail). It was he who discovered the mount left after the flood underneath which lay God's first temple built by Adam. And it was there that Abraham set out to rebuild the Ka'bah, which in its present form owes its origin to him.

Leaving his wife and child with some water and dates, Abraham left Mecca on God's command. Hagar suckled her son and they drank the remaining water. Soon, however, both faced great thirst and the child began to cry. Hagar began to run between two mounds named Safa and Marwah looking for water, repeating the journey seven times until an angel appeared to her, striking the ground with his wing, with the result that the spring of Zamzam, which Muslims consider as a "tributary" of the water of Paradise, gushed forth. Henceforth, Mecca was to be blessed with a source of water which has continued to this day. It was because of the Zamzam that the Jurhum tribe from northern Yemen came to settle in Mecca where they adopted Ishmael (Ismail), taught him Arabic and made him one of their own.

Muslim historians also believe that it was at Mount Thabir, situated north of the Mecca valley, that Abraham, upon returning to Mecca, took Ishmael (Ismail) to be sacrificed for God. In the Islamic version of the binding of the son of Abraham, the son himself was perfectly resigned to the Will of God as was the father. "So when they both surrendered [to Allah] and he had flung him upon his forehead We called out to him: 'O Abraham! Thou hast already fulfilled the vision.' Lo! Thus do We reward the good.... Then We ransomed him with a tremendous sacrifice. And we left for him among the later folk (the salvation): 'Peace be upon Abraham!'" (Qur'an, xxxvii: 103–9). This great episode of sacred history, shared in different versions by Jews, Christians and Muslims alike, is thus again associated by the Muslim mind with the area of Mecca.

It was after this event and the departure and return of Abraham to Mecca that the most lasting mark of the Patriarch in Mecca was created. Upon his return, Abraham discovered that his wife Hagar had died. Then he called upon his son Ishmael (Ismail), who is called "the father of the Arabs" and was the ancestor of the Prophet of Islam, to help him in the construction of the House of God, *bayt al-atiq* or the "Ancient House" as the Arabs called it. The Divine Peace (*al-sakinah*) descended in the form of a wind which brought a cloud in the shape of a dragon that revealed to them the site of the old temple. Abraham and Ishmael (Ismail) dug the ground until they discovered with awe the ancient temple built by Adam. A stone came to light on which there was the following inscription: "I am the God of Becca. I have created compassion and love as my two appellations. Whoever attains these virtues shall meet Me. And whoever removes himself from these virtues is removed from Me." Already Allah, whose Name is inseparable from the qualities of compassion and mercy in Islam and who was to reveal "Bismi'Llah al-Rahman al-Rahim" (In the Name of God, the Infinitely Good, the All-Merciful) as the formula of consecration in the Noble Qur'an, had spoken. And He had spoken at the place that was to become inseparable from the celebration of His Names of Rahman and Rahim from the time of the advent of Islam.

Abraham or Ibrahim, known in Islam also as Khalil Allah or Friend of God, built the Ka'bah as a sign of his perfect faith in his Friend. Thus does the Qur'an address him: "Associate naught with Me and purify My house for those who make the round (thereof) and those who stand and those who bow and make prostration. And proclaim unto mankind the Pilgrimage" (Qur'an, xxii: 26–7).

He made the first pilgrimage with his son Ishmael (Ismail), and in the presence of the archangel Gabriel performed all the elements which constitute the rite of Hajj today. Under Divine Command, he established a rite which was revived by the Prophet of Islam and which is inseparable from the reality of Mecca and its meaning for Muslims the world over to this day. Abraham was to leave Mecca to die in Palestine in al-Khalil, but he left an important part of himself and his heritage in Mecca. And so Abraham raised his hands in prayer and said according to the Noble Qur'an: "Our Lord, I have settled a part of my offspring in an infertile vale near Thy Sacred House, our Lord! That they may establish proper worship" (Qur'an, xiv: 37). Henceforth, Mecca became inseparable from Abrahamic monotheism, and despite the rise of Arabian paganism in later centuries in that city, it was finally here that the religion of the One was re-established in its final form with the advent of Islam. Mecca's sacred history links it therefore inalienably to the message and heritage of Abraham, whose progeny continued to live there. Eventually, they gained power over the city and finally, as a result of their indulgence in idolatry, lost that power because of the revelation of the message of the One to one of their own, namely, Muhammad— may blessings and peace be upon him—who destroyed the idols and renewed fully the monotheism of his ancestor Abraham.

The wilderness stretching to the north of Medina forms a striking contrast to the desert area lying at the center and east of the Arabian peninsula. The Hijaz region, in which both Mecca and Medina are located, has mountains extending both north and south, some continuing to be volcanically active.

The Protohistory of Arabia and the Holy Cities

Already in an inscription of the Assyrian King Salmanazar II, dating from 854 BC, there is reference to the "Arabs", probably meaning "desert dwellers". The Arabs were Semites who, with the help of camels, were able to navigate the Arabian peninsula around 1000 BC while creating settlements such as Aram and Eberin in the north of the peninsula. Divided into tribes, they guarded jealously their genealogy and tribal customs, and until the advent of Islam their allegiance was first and foremost to their tribe while intertribal skirmishes and warfare characterized their lives. Some of these tribes remained in a particular region while others, such as the Amaliq, mentioned in the Bible as the Amalekites, were to be found throughout the Arabian peninsula.

It was a branch of this tribe, known as the Abil, that founded the city of Yathrib, later to be known as Medina. Blessed by much underground water, the plain of Yathrib, lying between the ranges of the Sarat Mountains, became the site of a prosperous community. But its people disobeyed God and so were punished by natural calamities such as pestilence, and also the Prophet Moses sent an army to punish them. Centuries later, Jews, probably fleeing from Nebuchadnezzar, migrated to Yathrib and formed the community whose descendants the Prophet of Islam was to meet upon his migration to that city.

According to Arab custom going back to the earliest known historical period, it was forbidden to fight in the vicinity of the Ka'bah. Another branch of the Amaliq, taking advantage of the fact that the descendants of Ishmael (Ismail), the custodians of the Ka'bah, would not engage them in battle there, attacked them and drove them out. The descendants of Ismail took refuge in the gorges around Mecca as nomads, some wandering to other parts of Arabia and others remaining close to the House of God erected by their ancestors Abraham and Ishmael (Ismail). Gradually, Mecca grew in stature as the chief sanctuary of Arabia, and tribes would come from every corner of the peninsula to pray in and around the Ka'bah, which had by now become defiled, from the Islamic point of view, with idols of various tribes, the original significance of the structure as the House of the One God eclipsed and forgotten by the majority save the few who, however, remained attached to Abrahamic monotheism and whom Islam calls the *hunafa* or "primordialists". It was also as a result of the presence of these idols that Jews ceased to visit the Ka'bah. The structure of the Ka'bah remained unchanged, however, and it was rebuilt exactly as it was before by the Amaliq after a flood inundated and destroyed it. What changed over the centuries was that floods brought sedimentation from adjacent hills, which raised the ground around the Ka'bah to such an extent that the original mound upon which Abraham had built the Ka'bah was no longer visible.

It was the victory of the Jurhum tribe from the Yemen over the Amaliq and their conquest of Mecca that accentuated polytheism in the Sacred City. But they were, in turn, defeated by the Khuza'ah, an Arab tribe of Ismailite descent, which had migrated to the Yemen and then returned north. The Amaliq did not leave Mecca, however, without seeking to ravage it, including among their actions the burial of the spring of Zamzam. In entering Mecca, the Khuza'ah continued to protect the city as a center of pilgrimage for the Arab tribes, and themselves brought the famous idol Hubal, which they placed within the Ka'bah and which they made the chief idol of Mecca.

The Quraysh, the Hashimites and the Birth of the Prophet

Around the fourth or fifth Christian century, another Ismailite tribe, the Quraysh, one of whose members was to be chosen as the final prophet of God, began to gain ascendance in Mecca. One of their members, Qusayy, married the daughter of the chief of the Khuza'ah tribe and later became the ruler of Mecca and custodian of the Ka'bah. He ruled over both the Quraysh who lived near the sanctuary and those farther away. He was a capable ruler and it is said that it was he who built the city of Mecca in the form of concentric circles around the Ka'bah with the inhabitants of each circle being determined by their social rank, with those of higher rank living closer to the "Ancient House". This original plan of the city lasted into the historical period and traces could be found until the advent of the urban development of recent decades.

The grandson of Qusayy was named Hashim, after whom the clan of the Prophet, the Hashimite, is named. Hashim was also a competent ruler and succeeded in making Mecca prosperous by expanding trade routes through the city. He married Salma, one of the most influential women of Yathrib of the tribe of Khazraj, and from this union was born Shaybah. Brought up originally by his mother in Yathrib, he was taken to Mecca upon the death of his father by his uncle Muttalib. Since he was riding behind his uncle in entering the city, he was called in error Abd al-Muttalib (the slave of

Muttalib), a name with which he came to be identified. This remarkable figure of great spiritual stature and statesmanship finally became the ruler of Mecca.

Once, while sleeping by the area adjacent to the Ka'bah known as Hijr Ismail, he dreamt that he should dig for the spring of Zamzam buried long before by the Amaliq. The dream occurred twice, and so Abd al-Muttalib began to circumambulate the Ka'bah. After completing this ancient ritual, he saw a number of birds strutting to a place a hundred yards away from the Ka'bah. And so he began to dig in that spot to which he was led by the sign from Heaven. Soon, the long-lost spring of Zamzam gushed forth as if foretelling of the reassertion of primordial monotheism and the reconsecration of the Ka'bah to the One in the near future. The tribe of Hashim was given the right of supervision over the water of the Zamzam, a privilege whose significance can hardly be overemphasized.

Abd al-Muttalib had vowed that if he were to have ten sons, he would sacrifice one of them to God to whom he, as a *hanif*, always prayed, never bowing before the idols of Mecca. After the drawing of lots, Abd Allah, his most beloved son, was chosen for sacrifice but his mother, Fatimah, from the powerful Makhzum tribe, was opposed to this act. After much consultation and prayer, Abd al-Muttalib agreed to sacrifice a hundred camels instead. The future father of the Prophet of Islam was thereby saved and Abd Allah who, because of his physical beauty was called the Joseph of his time, was married in 569 according to his father's choice to Aminah, a descendant of the brother of Qusayy.

There lived at that time a *hanif* in Mecca by the name of Waraqah who had become a Christian. A holy man in touch with other Christians of the region, he declared that the coming of a new prophet was imminent. The rabbis had also believed in this news but they considered the new prophet to be a descendant of Isaac while Waraqah thought that he could be an Arab. Before the marriage ceremony, as Abd Allah and his father Abd al-Muttalib were walking toward the place where the ceremony was to take place, the beautiful and pious sister of Waraqah, Qutaylah, was standing at the door of her house. She saw Abd Allah and became startled by the light in his face which she knew to be the light of prophecy. She

The Mosque of the Prophet with its green dome built in 678/1279. The color green is associated with the Blessed Prophet and his family, and the green dome has become since the last century, along with the Ka'bah, a global symbol of Islam.

offered herself in marriage to him for the hundred camels that were sacrificed by his father in his place, but Abd Allah could not disobey his father and therefore refused the offer. After the consummation of the marriage, the next day when Abd Allah saw Qutaylah again she showed no interest in him, and when he asked the cause she said that the light in his face had disappeared. That light was to manifest itself in the being of the child who was conceived the night before. But Abd Allah did not live long enough to see his son Muhammad, who was born in the Year of the Elephant, that is 570, as an orphan.

That year was indeed a momentous one for Mecca, Arabia and ultimately most of the world. The Christian ruler of Abyssinia, Abrahah, had conquered the Yemen and built a cathedral in San'a with the hope that this monument would replace Mecca as the center of religious activity in Arabia, but the cathedral was defiled by a member of the Kinanah tribe who managed to escape to safety. Abrahah thus decided to take revenge upon Mecca by razing the Ka'bah to the ground. He assembled a vast army with an elephant leading in front. Approaching Mecca, he asked for the leader of the Quraysh to come out to meet him, saying that he had nothing against the people of the city but wanted only to destroy the Ka'bah. Abd al-Muttalib came out to meet him, and to the great surprise of the latter did not ask for the Ka'bah to be saved but only for his camels, taken by Abrahah's soldiers, to be given back. When Abrahah asked why this was his only demand, Abd al-Muttalib said that he was responsible only for his camels and that the Lord of the

A rare photograph of the Ka'bah taken in 1941 when an unusual deluge in an ordinarily very dry region covered the entire area around the Ka'bah, which stands on lower ground than most of the other mosques in the ravine of Mecca.

Ka'bah would take care of his own House. Abd al-Muttalib then returned to the Ka'bah, asking God for help and then left with all the Meccans to the adjacent hills.

Abrahah then decided to march upon Mecca, but near the city the elephant in front of the army refused to move and simply sat on the ground. No amount of beating could change its will. Suddenly, the sky turned black and a cloud of birds appeared, which pelted the army, killing most of the soldiers, the rest fleeing back to the Yemen. Hence the year, so famous in Islamic sources, became known as the Year of the Elephant. As a result, Mecca, which was soon to enter into the full light of history, was saved and the Quraysh gained greater respect among the other tribes as the people of God because their prayers were answered.

The momentous nature of this year was not only, however, in the miraculous saving of the Ka'bah, but most of all in the birth of the person who, forty years later, would be visited by the archangel Gabriel in Mecca and who would rid the Ka'bah of all the dross of forgetfulness of the One which, over the centuries, had covered its original face. Muhammad ibn Abd Allah—upon whom be blessings and peace—was born to Aminah in Mecca and was given this name by God's command. His grandfather, Abd al-Muttalib, took the new-born child to the Ka'bah where he offered prayers to God. Thus, the life and later message of the Prophet became intertwined with the Ka'bah from the earliest moments of his earthly life and a link was established which, according to Islam, will last until the Day of Judgement.

The Prophet in Mecca and Medina

The life of the Prophet of Islam was spent nearly completely in the two holy cities of Mecca and Medina where his *barakah* is ubiquitous for pious Muslims to this day. It was in Mecca that he was nurtured and raised, while spending some time in the care of the nomadic tribes in the areas around the city as was the tradition of the time. It was in Mecca that he gained fame as a just and trustworthy person and was bestowed with the title of al-Amin, the Trusted One, even before being chosen as prophet. It was in this city that he married Khadijah and where his children were born. In fact, the foundations of his house were visible in Mecca until the recent expansions of the Great Mosque. It was from here that he led the caravans of Khadijah, his wealthy and faithful wife, to Syria and back. It was in the hills around this city that he took refuge to be alone with God, and it was on the top of one of these hills, al-Hira, which stands just outside today's Mecca, that in the year 610 he was visited by the archangel Gabriel and the first verses of the Noble Qur'an were revealed to him.

The advent of the revelation, of course, transformed the life of the Prophet completely, placing upon his shoulders the responsibility of establishing God's religion based upon the doctrine of Divine Unity (*al-tawhid*) amidst a society given to idolatry and in a tribe which derived its power from idol worship. Although his message was accepted immediately by his beloved wife Khadijah, trusted friend Abu Bakr, and intimate cousin and future son-in- law Ali, it was in the middle of his own city of Mecca that the Prophet was to encounter the most severe challenges, opposition, humiliation and threats, and experience the bitterness of being the object of enmity of so many of the members of his own Quraysh tribe. But also it was here that he persevered and succeeded in creating the nucleus of the first Islamic society.

It was also from the blessed city of Mecca that God chose to have him ascend during the Nocturnal Journey (*al-miraj*) with the help of the archangel Gabriel, from Mecca to Jerusalem and from Jerusalem to the Divine Throne. Jerusalem was the first direction of prayer for Muslims (*al-qiblah al-ula*) and then, while the Prophet was in Mecca, God ordered that city to become the *qiblah*. The *miraj* reconfirmed for all later generations of Muslims the spiritual connection between Jerusalem and Mecca, the first and second *qiblah* and the center of monotheism as a whole and Islamic monotheism respectively; two cities whose spiritual reality will, according to Islamic teachings, become reunited at the end of time, while being deeply interconnected here and now.

The Prophet was to leave a Mecca in deep enmity against him, where even his life was now threatened, for the hospitality of the city which was to take his name and become known as the City of the Prophet, Madinat al-nabi. He was to return to his city of birth several years later to perform the pilgrimage in peace and finally to enter Mecca in triumph in the moment which marked the crowning achievement of his earthly life. He was to order Ali and Bilal to rid the Ka'bah of the idols of the Age of Ignorance (*al-jahiliyyah*) and to re-establish it as the primordial temple dedicated to the One God. His final departure from Mecca left that city as the unquestionable center of the new religious universe created by the Qur'anic revelation. At once the site of the Ka'bah, the birthplace of the Prophet, the place of the first revelation of the Qur'an and the *qiblah* of all Muslims, Mecca thus became and remains the holiest of Islamic cities.

It was, however, the city of Yathrib to the north that opened its arms to the Prophet at a moment when his life and that of the nascent Islamic community were threatened by the intractable enmity of the Quraysh in Mecca. The Prophet thus set out with his trusted companion Abu Bakr for what was to become Medina, having sent his followers, known as *al-muhajirun*, literally "the immigrants", in small groups before him to that city with a few to follow afterwards. It was at the outskirts of Medina, at the site of the present Quba Mosque, where he performed his prayers. It was to the present site of this mosque that his camel was to take him—by its own will so as to avoid contention between different groups that wanted to offer him hospitality at their homes.

Medina was integrated by the Prophet into the first fully fledged Islamic society, to become henceforth the model for all later Islamic societies. The Prophet had a Constitution prepared for the city which is the earliest Islamic political document. Here, he established norms which were to become models for later Islamic practice and promulgated laws which became foundational to Islamic Law or al-Shari'ah. While the revelation continued in Medina, the community became transformed from a small number of scattered adherents to a fully organized society, the heart of a vast religious universe which was in the process of formation. But the challenge of Meccan forces against Islam continued and Medina and its environs were witness to crucial battles which decided the fate of the new community. The first great battle (*al-ghazz*) was al-Badr, in which a vastly outnumbered Muslim army overcame the Meccan army with the help of angels, according to traditional sources, at a site just outside of Medina. The battle of Uhud, in which the Muslims were defeated and the Prophet injured without the Meccans pursuing their victory, likewise took place close to the present limits of the city, while the site of the battle of Khaybar, in which Ali showed exemplary valor, is not far away. Medina was even besieged once and saved only by the wise decision of Salman al-Farsi, the first Persian to embrace Islam, to dig a ditch around the city, hence the name of the battle as al-Khandaq or "the Ditch".

It was in and around Medina that both successes and failures took place militarily as well as socially and politically, but while the failures were shortlived and overcome by never-ending hope and reliance of the Prophet upon God, the successes increased and the strength of the Islamic community augmented from day to day until gradually all of Arabia became united under the banner of Islam during the lifetime of the Prophet, with Medina serving as the sociopolitical capital and center of this newly integrated world. The man who rode with his close friend Abu Bakr from Mecca to the city of Yathrib became within a decade in that city, which had now become Medina, the prophet-king of the whole of Arabia and the founder of a new religious civilization and society whose boundaries were to stretch in less than a century from China to France. And it was to this city, in which God had bequeathed upon him the mastery and dominion of a whole world, that he returned from his city

A pilgrim from Nigeria praying by the door of
the Mosque of the Prophet. Barring exceptional
circumstances, such as an epidemic, the Nigerians
constitute the largest body of pilgrims from Africa.

This group of women pilgrims from Kerala in Southern India wear this distinctive blue color to distinguish them from others so that the members of the group do not become lost amidst the vast crowds.

of birth, Mecca, to spend the last few months of his life. Furthermore, it was there in Medina that he died in 10/632 to be buried in his own apartment next to the mosque which he had ordered to be built, the Masjid al-nabi or Mosque of the Prophet, that is the prototype of all later mosques. Medina, therefore, became the second sacred city of Islam, reflecting to this day, and despite the loss in recent years of much of its traditional architecture and palm groves (some planted by Ali and other companions of the Prophet), crucial stages in the life of the Prophet, his family and companions. One can still sense the perfume of his presence in that beautiful oasis city, al-Madinah, which Muslims cherish the world over.

Mecca and Medina in Later History

Through all the later vicissitudes of Islamic history, Mecca and Medina have continued as the spiritual and religious centers of the Islamic world, but the political heart of the Islamic world was to leave Arabia a little more than two decades after the death of the Prophet. Abu Bakr, Umar and Uthman, the first three caliphs, ruled the ever-expanding Islamic world from Medina, where they enlarged the Mosque of the Prophet as well as the limits of the city itself. But the fourth caliph, Ali, facing the rebellion of the garrison in Syria, moved to Kufa in Iraq to prepare an army to put down this revolt. His coming to Kufa, which henceforth became the capital until Ali's assassination, moved the political center of Islam out of Arabia forever. For after Ali, the Umayyads who gained political power did not return to Mecca or Medina but made Damascus their capital while their successors, the Abbasids, built Baghdad as their capital. Both dynasties, however, influenced the architecture of the two holy cities. During the early Umayyad period, the people of both Mecca and Medina resisted strongly Umayyad directives. The grandson of Abu Bakr, Abd Allah, led a revolt in Mecca against the Umayyads, as a result of which the Ka'bah became seriously damaged and was rebuilt with the help of architects and craftsmen using Yemeni building techniques. But the city was attacked again by the Umayyad general al-Hajjaj and all of Abd Allah's work on the Ka'bah was destroyed and the monument reconstructed. Likewise in Medina, many of the houses of the *ahl al-bayt* or household of the Prophet, including the house of Fatimah, were destroyed by the Umayyads. Some people believe, in fact, that the Umayyads built the monumental mosques of Jerusalem and Damascus so that Muslims would pay less attention to Mecca and Medina, but such was not to be the case.

Although raids and skirmishes continued from time to time, the most famous being that of the Carmathians in the fourth/tenth century during which they stole the Black Stone of the Ka'bah for twenty-one years, Mecca and Medina continued to be revered as the spiritual centers of the Islamic world. They even resisted the more worldly art that the Umayyads had developed farther north and had sought to impose upon the two holy cities. During the Abbasid as well as Mamluk and Ottoman periods, great attention continued to be paid to the two cities and many fine monuments were created, some of which survive to this day, for it was the greatest honor and responsibility to be custodian and protector of the two holy cities. Since 1926, after the demise of the Ottoman Empire and the defeat of the Hashimites of Mecca by the Saudis, Hijaz has been a part of Saudi Arabia. Under the new situation, the custodianship of the two holy cities continued to be seen as the greatest honor by the Saudis to the extent that the King of Saudi Arabia is not referred to as "His Majesty" but as "Custodian of the Two Holy Mosques".

During all the centuries of Islamic history, Mecca and Medina remained outside the major turmoils in the heartland of the Islamic world farther north. The tremors of the Crusades and the Mongol invasion hardly reached them, while they continued to be visited by streams of pilgrims from the east to the west of the Islamic world, many of whom, in fact, took refuge in the calm and peace of these cities from either turmoil in their place of birth, or the din of the life of the world, as we see in the case of Baha al-Din Walad, the father of Jalal al-Din Rumi who, fleeing the Mongol invasion in Khurasan, came with his young son to Mecca before settling in Anatolia; or Imam al-Ghazali, who spent years in seclusion in the holy cities. Many of those Islamic scholars, who are called Makki or Madani, hailed, in fact, from other regions of the Islamic world but settled in the two holy cities. These cities remained over the centuries as the heart of Islamic civilization whose more evident and well-known centers as far as political, intellectual and artistic life are concerned, lay north, east and west of the sacred land of Hijaz, the birthplace of Islam. Hijaz itself continues to this day to be the religious center of the Islamic world as a result of the ever-living presence and continuing significance of Mecca and Medina.

The Ka'bah

This House of God and primordial temple dedicated to the One, which is the object of the Hajj and the focal point for the daily prayers or the *qiblah* of all Muslims, stands at the heart of Mecca as testimony to the nature of Islam as the pure mono-theism which revived the monotheism of Abraham and ultimately the primordial message of unity revealed to Adam, at once the father of humanity and first prophet. The Ka'bah is the concrete symbol of the origin of Islam and, in Muslim eyes, of all religion. To come to the Ka'bah is to return to one's origin. But it is also the supreme center of Islam by virtue of which all Muslims turn to it in their daily canonical prayers. Like all veritable traditional civilizations, Islam is dominated by the two realities of Origin and Center, and these two fundamental dimensions of Islamic life are present in the Ka'bah. Throughout his or her life on earth, a Muslim, whether living by one of the volcanic peaks of Java or in the desert of Mauritania, is aware of the Ka'bah as the point on earth which links him or her to the origin of himself or herself, of his or her religion, Islam, and ultimately of humanity as such. The Muslim is also aware that all points of space on earth are linked by an invisible line to a unique center which is the Ka'bah towards which one directs one's face five times a day in prayer. The Muslim, therefore, has a relation to the Ka'bah which is at once static and dynamic, static for there is a constant link between every point of the space of the Islamic cosmos and the Ka'bah, and dynamic because it is toward the Ka'bah that one journeys during the pilgrimage. In a sense, the daily prayers (*al-salah*) represent that static relation and the Hajj the dynamic one. Together they confirm the overwhelming and majestic presence of the Ka'bah as at once Origin and Center in the Islamic religious universe, not because of the Ka'bah in its earthly reality but because of what it signifies as the House of God, for in reality it is God alone who is the Origin and Center of a Muslim's life.

A scene of Arafat photographed during the Hajj in 1885. The photo, taken by the Dutch orientalist Snouck Hurgronje, whose Muslim name was Abd al-Ghaffar, shows a number of pilgrims around the Mount of Mercy (Jabal al-Rahmah) at the center.

The Ka'bah is considered by Muslims to be a reflection here below of the celestial temple surrounding God's Throne (*al-arsh*) except that by inverse analogy, here below, one can speak of surrounding the Throne while in the principal domain it is the Throne that surrounds all things as the Qur'an asserts. The archaic nature of the Ka'bah points to its primordial character. Being a cube (hence the name Ka'bah which means "cube" in Arabic) or almost a cube, it is 12 meters long, 10 meters broad and 16 meters high, possessing therefore dimensions which are in harmonic relation with each other according to the Pythagorean meaning of harmony. As a cube, the Ka'bah also symbolizes the stability and immutability that characterize Islam itself, a religion based on harmony, stability and immutability in its basic reality, hence the truth that Islam can be renewed but not reformed. It is of interest to note that the Holy of Holies in Jerusalem, in which the Ark of the Covenant was kept, was also in the form of a cube. And like the ark, the Ka'bah is considered to reflect the Presence of God. It is like a living body; hence its being dressed in the black cloth (*al-kiswah*), with golden Qur'anic verses. This dressing of the Sacred House of God, an old Semitic tradition not found in the Graeco-Roman world, is renewed every year and the old *kiswah* is cut up and distributed so as to allow the *barakah* of the Ka'bah to emanate among those to whom pieces of the cloth are given. From the earliest centuries of Islamic history, the *kiswah* was made in Egypt and carried with great care to Mecca, but now it is made near the holy city itself.

The Ka'bah is a structure with cosmic and even metacosmic significance. It lies on the axis which unites Heaven and Earth in the Islamic cosmos. It is situated at the hub of the world at the point of intersection between the *axis mundi* and the earth. Its properties reflect cosmic harmony. Its four corners point to the four cardinal directions which represent the four pillars (*al-arkan*) of the traditional cosmos. As for the Black Stone (*al-hajar al-aswad*) at its corner, it is a meteorite, therefore from beyond the earthly ambience. Abraham (Ibrahim) and Ishmael (Ismail) are said to have brought it from the hill of Abu Qubays near Mecca where it had been preserved since coming to earth. According to the Prophet, the stone had descended from Heaven whiter than milk but turned black as the result of the sins of the children of Adam although something of its original luminosity survives. The stone also symbolizes the original covenant made, according to the Qur'an, between God and Adam and all his progeny, whereby all members of humanity accepted on that "pre-eternal moment" (*al-azal*), when the covenant was made, the Lordship of God.

The communal prayer around the Ka'bah is the most tangible sign of perfect submission to God's Will as the circumambulation around it marks the return of man to his original Edenic perfection. By emptying the Ka'bah of the idols, the Prophet not only reconsecrated the Primordial Temple as the House of the One God but also taught all Muslims that in order to be truly Muslim they must empty the heart, which is the microcosmic counterpart of the Ka'bah, of all idols, of all that is other than God, making the heart worthy of receiving the Divine Presence.

The Ka'bah is a form, yet the symbol of the formless. It is protoarchitecture, yet the source of all Islamic architecture. The black color of the *kiswah* is the symbol of that darkness which is none other than the intensity of light, the color beyond all colors which contains all colors, all forms. The golden letters of the Noble Qur'an embellishing it are the evident manifestation of the Divine Essence from which the Word originates in the golden color of the sun, itself symbol of the Divine Intellect. The black and gold reveal the relation between the Word in the manifested world (*al-shahadah*) and the Unmanifested to which the Qur'an refers so often as the Invisible (*al-ghayb*).

To stand before the Ka'bah is to behold the miracle of manifestation in relation to its invisible Source in revelation as well as in creation which is also God's primordial revelation. That is why the Ka'bah is at once the House of God, the center of the Islamic cosmic ambience and an outward symbol of the heart of God's slave, man, the heart which when purified reveals its true nature, according to the famous saying (*hadith*) of the Blessed Prophet, as the Throne of the Compassionate (*al-Rahman*, which is a Name of the Divine Essence).

The Pilgrimage (al-Hajj)

Life itself is not only a journey but in reality a pilgrimage, whether man is aware of it or not, for at the end of the journey of life stands the gate of death and encounter with the Sacred, in the same way that the journey of the pilgrim leads him to the sacred precinct which is the very goal and purpose of the journey. Islam has taken this essential truth and made it an integral element of the religious life by making the pilgrimage to Mecca obligatory. But pilgrimage to more local sites is also part and parcel of the life of traditional Muslims. Whether it be Mulay Idris in Morocco, Ra's al-Husayn in Cairo, the Dome of the Rock in Jerusalem, numerous sites in Iraq and Iran, such as Najaf, Karbala, Samarrah and Kazimayn, Mashhad and Qom, all revered especially by Shi'ites, or the mausoleums of Dadaji Ganjbaksh in Lahore and Mu'in al-Din Chisti in Ajmer in India, all these sites, to which pilgrimage is made by millions of the faithful annually, are reflections of the holy cities of Mecca and Medina. The grace (*barakah*) of these sacred precincts thus flows to the other regions of the Islamic world like blood which, issuing from the heart, reaches all the limbs of the body. It is not accidental that all these sites are associated with events in the life of the Prophet and his household or are mausoleums of those who were either biological or spiritual children of the founder of Islam.

These forms of pilgrimage are, however, but echoes to loci of sacred presence, of the supreme pilgrimage which is the Hajj, one of the obligatory pillars of Islam. The Hajj recapitulates the whole spiritual journey of man on earth. As the rite instituted by Abraham in commemoration of the One God of pure monotheism and revived by the Prophet, every part of it goes back to Prophetic example and his wonts (*sunnah*).

The sunset (*maghrib*) prayers at the Prophet's Mosque in Medina during the week before the annual season of the Hajj when a large number of pilgrims assemble in Medina. The picture shows female pilgrims in an adjacent garden of the mosque.

The performance of the Hajj, which countless Muslim men and women have undertaken over the centuries, coming in heat and cold from near and far, on foot or on camels, in boats or on horses, from high mountain valleys or distant islands, is itself a *jihad* or exertion in the path of God. It implies sacrifice and hardship, leading sometimes, even in the present age of so-called modern convenience, to death which Muslims espouse with open arms for they are then promised the death of a martyr and entry into Paradise if their intentions have been pure.

It is enough to understand the real significance of each of the elements of the Hajj, to grasp the transforming power of this unique rite which unites Muslims from all over the world once a year before the majestic presence of the House of God. In approaching the holy precinct (*al-haram*), whose boundaries were delineated by the Prophet, the pilgrim must perform the complete ritual ablution (*al-ghusl*) to wash away the impurities of worldly existence. Each pilgrim must then put on the *ihram*, two pieces of seamless white cloth, so as to be in a consecrated state. Henceforth the pilgrim must abstain from all evil thoughts and the cares of the world and also from gratification of sexual passions. The men and women who are to perform the Hajj in this state must die to the world, and the white color of the *ihram* does not only signify purity but also spiritual death. That is why most pilgrims put their *ihram* away at the end of the pilgrimage to be used for their shroud, which in Islam is also always white. The *ihram* also signifies primordial man's "nakedness" in standing before God, as all Muslims will do on the Day of Judgement.

Upon entering Mecca, the pilgrims must make the circumambulation (*al-tawaf*) around the Ka'bah seven times and try to kiss the *hajar al-aswad* at its corner. The movement of the circumambulation is counter-clockwise, for in performing this rite man reverses the process of the fall and all the imperfections which he has accrued within himself as a result of the consequences of the downward flow of time. The circumambulations reintegrate the men and women who actualize the meaning of the rite within themselves into the Edenic state, in that condition in which all the children of Adam bore testimony to God's Oneness. The kissing of the Black Stone is, in a

Expansions to the Holy Mosque in Mecca

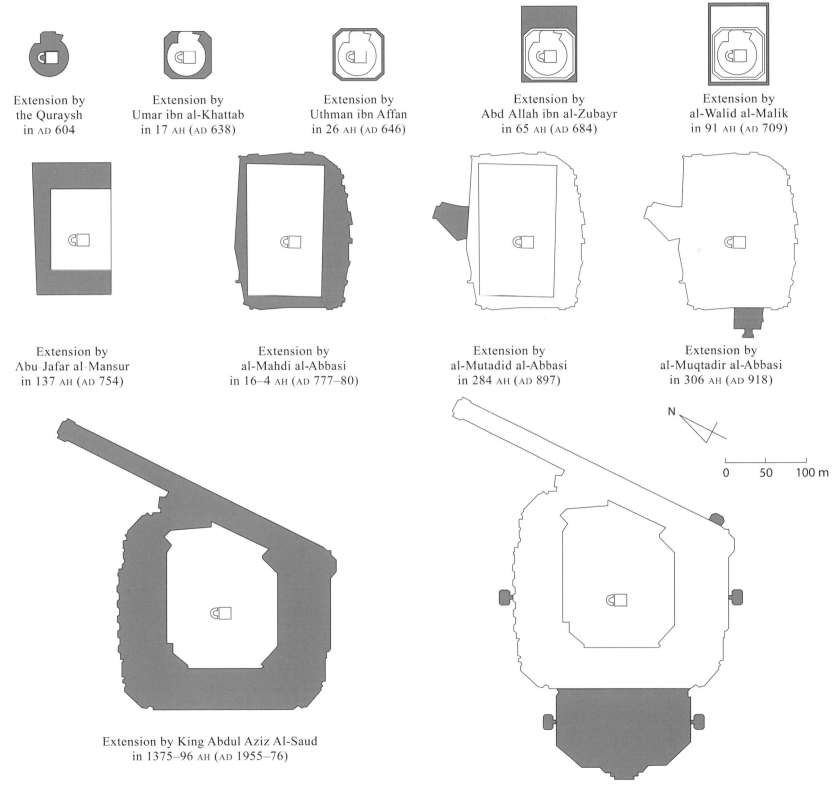

Extension by
the Quraysh
in AD 604

Extension by
Umar ibn al-Khattab
in 17 AH (AD 638)

Extension by
Uthman ibn Affan
in 26 AH (AD 646)

Extension by
Abd Allah ibn al-Zubayr
in 65 AH (AD 684)

Extension by
al-Walid al-Malik
in 91 AH (AD 709)

Extension by
Abu-Jafar al-Mansur
in 137 AH (AD 754)

Extension by
al-Mahdi al-Abbasi
in 16–4 AH (AD 777–80)

Extension by
al-Mutadid al-Abbasi
in 284 AH (AD 897)

Extension by
al-Muqtadir al-Abbasi
in 306 AH (AD 918)

N

0   50   100 m

Extension by King Abdul Aziz Al-Saud
in 1375–96 AH (AD 1955–76)

Extension by the Custodian of the Two Holy Mosques,
King Fahd, in 1409–16 AH (AD 1988–95)

39

A postcard of Medina (date unknown) shows that the city had grown in comparison with the map on page 12.

sense, the renewal of the pre-eternal covenant (*al-mithaq*) with God. Furthermore, in relation to that Edenic perfection, outward distinctions are irrelevant; hence the performance of the Hajj in a dress which is the same for all, whether king or beggar, for in the sight of God "the noblest of you ... is the best in conduct" (Qur'an, xlix: 13) and outward social and class distinctions play no role. In making the *tawaf* amidst a vast sea of humanity, black, white and yellow, Arab and non-Arab, dark haired and blond, without awareness of a person's wealth or position in society, one gains a glimpse of the reality that the only basic distinction of human beings before God is their inner purity and spiritual character, while in the realm of creation there are diversities of race, age, gender, language and culture, which are themselves willed by God. The *tawaf* reveals a unity in diversity which is overwhelming and at the very antipode of a quantitative egalitarianism which mistakes uniformity for unity.

The *sa'y* or rapid walk between Safa and Marwah, celebrating the rapid movement of Hagar and her son Ishmael (Ismail) in quest of water, which appeared miraculously in the form of the sacred spring of Zamzam, represents our quest in this world for the life-bestowing bounties of God and His Mercy which fulfills our quest. The spring of Zamzam itself is an earthly "tributary" flowing from the springs of Paradise. Its water heals body and soul and is brought back by pilgrims and distributed throughout the Islamic world as a blessing. It is one of the most precious gifts that a pilgrim can bring back to his family and friends.

The events outside of Mecca are intimately related to sacred history and eschatological realities. The great plain of Arafat, where all the pilgrims assemble in a vast congregation and where the deepest prayers are offered for the forgiveness of one's sins as well as the welfare of others, symbolizes the plain of Mahshar or Resurrection when everyone will stand before God on the Day of Judgement denuded of all accessories and paraphernalia, with one's only possession being one's actions in this world and the effect they have had upon the soul. In the middle of Arafat stands Jabal al-Rahmah or the Mount of Mercy, where the last verses of the Noble Qur'an were revealed and where one of the famous farewell addresses of the Blessed Prophet was delivered. It is here that the alchemy of union between various aspects of human nature takes place and men and women regain their primordial wholeness, for it was in the plain of Arafat that Adam and Eve are said to have found each other again after their fall on earth from Paradise. All of us, whether male or female, contain the two poles of the human reality symbolized by Adam and Eve within ourselves. But these two poles, representing our active and passive natures and tendencies, are now in discord. The alchemical wedding, whose fruit is gold or the perfection of the soul, is none other than the harmonious wedding between the Adam and Eve of our soul, a wedding which can become actualized, for those aware of the profound significance of the rites of the Hajj, at the great plain of Arafat where in sacred history such a union took place on the objective plane at the dawn of our earthly existence.

It is at Mina, where the Prophet delivered his last eloquent words during his final pilgrimage, that pilgrims cast stones against pillars representing Satan (*al-Shaytan*). This rite is, however, not only an external act but also an external support for the inner battle with the demon within, a battle that must be carried out incessantly until final victory. Muslims usually begin ritual actions, including recitation of the Qur'an, by taking refuge in God from the accursed Satan which in the Arabic formula, *al-Shaytan al-rajim*, means literally Satan against whom the stone is cast. The ritual at Mina actualizes, in a scene which is unforgettable for those who participate in it, a reality of human life of which we must be always aware no matter what our religious and spiritual accomplishments, that reality being the need for the constant battle against the forces of evil and dispersion within the soul. This unforgettable experience remains a powerful weapon in the journey of life, one which those pilgrims who make the rites with pure intention and devotion will never forget.

Finally, there is the sacrifice of an animal in emulation of the sacrifice of Abraham, the flesh of the sacrificed animals being given to the poor. Like Judaism, Islam obliges its followers to slaughter ritually those animals which are permitted by religious Law to eat, sacrificing them before God. The sacrifice at the end of the Hajj not only reasserts the significance of this Islamic practice but also symbolizes the sacrifice of the soul before God, for the greatest sacrifice that we can make before God is that of our carnal and passionate soul. It was to this battle, to overcome the lower soul, that the Blessed Prophet referred as *al-jihad al-akbar* or greater exertion upon the path of God, in comparison to ordinary *jihad*, to defend Islam and its borders to which he referred, upon returning from the battle of Badr that determined the future of the newly born religious community, as the lesser *jihad* or *al-jihad al-asghar*.

The rite of sacrifice is so significant that the great celebration at the end of the Hajj is called the Feast of Sacrifice (Id al-adha or Id-i-qurban in Persian). But it must be remembered that the root of the word *adha* possesses another meaning, which is that of clarity and lucidity and is related by certain Muslim writers to the Day of Resurrection. This meaning of the term is also mysteriously present at the end of the Hajj, for the pilgrim has now been washed of his or her sins and begins life anew, resurrected as a potentially perfect servant of God. The final farewell visit to the Ka'bah is to seal the remembrance of the Center and the new life it has given to the pilgrim who is now called a *hajji* (male) or *hajjiyah* (female). That is why when the pilgrim returns home, everyone comes to visit him or her to gain something of the *barakah* of the Center and the purity of the pilgrim born into a new life which must now be an exemplar of righteousness, piety and virtue.

Caravans of pilgrims with palanquins on camels go through Medina.

The Holy Cities Today

Modern methods of transportation have increased the number of pilgrims greatly during the past few decades. Some two million people now make the annual pilgrimage, coming from all over the traditional areas of the Islamic world as well as from Western Europe, North and South America and Australia where the presence of Islamic communities is more recent. One can now see pilgrims from Los Angeles, Caracas and London as well as Dakar, Baku, Samarqand and Jakarta—not to speak of the central areas of the Islamic world. This vast increase in the number of pilgrims has caused the Great Mosque at Mecca and the Mosque of the Prophet to be expanded immensely but at the cost of the destruction of many quarters around the two sacred areas, quarters which contained historic houses and were scenes of many of the events of the sacred history of Islam.

What is remarkable is that despite the ravages of modernism, the rite instituted by the Patriarch Abraham and re-established by the Prophet of Islam continues as a unique event in today's world. Every year during the lunar Islamic month of Dhu al-hijjah, pilgrims come to Mecca and also visit Medina. The image described in traditional sources of Mecca as a womb which once a year grows immensely and is then emptied still holds but one must add that the Great Mosque is now never empty. Now, throughout the whole year outside of the season for the annual Hajj, many Muslims make the pilgrimage to the two holy cities to perform the lesser pilgrimage which is called *al-umrah*, and even in the middle of the night throughout the year thousands can be seen circumambulating around the Ka'bah in a constantly moving circle of humanity crying "labbayka allahumma labbayk" (at Thy service, O Lord, at Thy service). To behold such a site with its constancy day and night, season after season, is to see the earthly reflection of the heavens rotating around the solar star and, according to the Qur'an, praising God constantly.

The Hajj remains, as in the days of old, also the occasion for the purchase and exchange of gifts and of ideas, some historians of science having called the Hajj of the earlier centuries the first international conference on the sciences. The Hajj continues to be, moreover, a powerful means for various parts of the Islamic community (*al-ummah*) to know each other and therefore is instrumental in the integration of the community. But despite all the outward changes related to communication, facilities and the like, the Hajj remains first and foremost what it has always been, a return to our Center and Origin, a death and rebirth, a spiritual rejuvenation and a renewal of our pre-eternal covenant with God. It remains a powerful way, along with other Islamic rites, of realizing the Unity of God (*al-tawhid*), and in the light of that unity the interrelation of all of His creation. That is why Mecca and its twin city Medina flourish as the heart and sacred Center of the Islamic universe and will continue to do so as long as there are men and women who accept the truth of "la ilaha illa'Llah" and "Muhammadun rasul Allah", whose hearts palpitate with the rhythms of the psalmody of the Noble Qur'an and whose minds and souls remain nourished by the message of the Noble Book first revealed in Mecca to a man who was born in that city and who died in Medina, the man with whom the cycle of prophecy for present humanity came to a close.

"Wa'l-hamdu li'Llah wahdahu"
(All praise belongs to God in His Oneness)

Expansions to the Prophet's Mosque in Medina

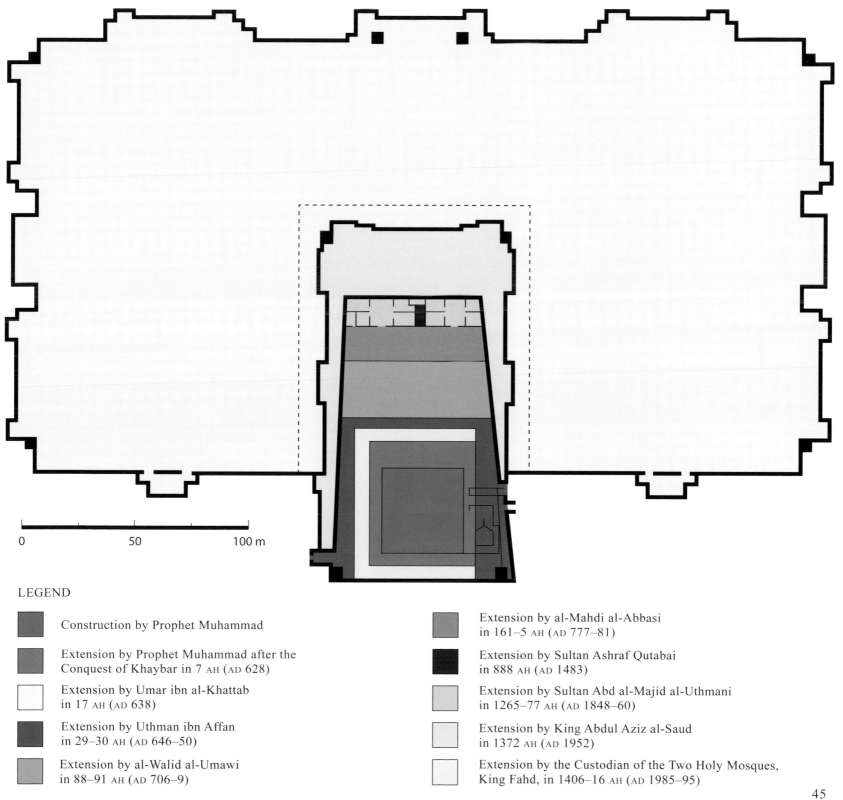

0   50   100 m

LEGEND

■ Construction by Prophet Muhammad

■ Extension by Prophet Muhammad after the Conquest of Khaybar in 7 AH (AD 628)

□ Extension by Umar ibn al-Khattab in 17 AH (AD 638)

■ Extension by Uthman ibn Affan in 29–30 AH (AD 646–50)

■ Extension by al-Walid al-Umawi in 88–91 AH (AD 706–9)

■ Extension by al-Mahdi al-Abbasi in 161–5 AH (AD 777–81)

■ Extension by Sultan Ashraf Qutabai in 888 AH (AD 1483)

■ Extension by Sultan Abd al-Majid al-Uthmani in 1265–77 AH (AD 1848–60)

□ Extension by King Abdul Aziz al-Saud in 1372 AH (AD 1952)

□ Extension by the Custodian of the Two Holy Mosques, King Fahd, in 1406–16 AH (AD 1985–95)

Mecca the Blessed

Here is the heart of the Islamic world, and even the Islamic cosmos by virtue of containing at its center the Ka'bah, the point where the world axis of the Islamic universe connecting Heaven and earth touches our human world. This is the city upon whose soil Abraham and Ismail (Ishmael) walked, in one of whose precincts the most perfect creature of God, Muhammad ibn Abd Allah— may God's blessings and peace be upon him—was born, in whose vicinity God revealed the first verses of the Noble Qur'an. It was here that the earliest Islamic community was born and where the Prophet experienced his greatest trials and triumphs. Its streets were traversed by the great companions, such as Abu Bakr, Umar and Uthman, while Ali was born in the Ka'bah at the heart of the city. The house of the Prophet where Fatimah was born stood in Mecca until only recently. Are there other cities which have produced so many figures who transformed world history? And then there are all those great Islamic scholars, scientists, theologians, philosophers and Sufi saints who have visited Mecca over the ages. Their spirit seems to hover over the city as does the spirit of all the great men of action who came as humble pilgrims to its doors.

The prayer of sunset (*maghrib*) performed at the Grand Mosque in Mecca shortly before the annual Hajj when some two million pilgrims gather in that city. The steep and craggy rock mountain beyond the Ka'bah is Mount Hira. At the top of it is located the cave in which the Blessed Prophet received the first Qur'anic revelation.

ABOVE AND RIGHT This gateway, designed as a Qur'an holder, stands over the main highway connecting Jeddah to Mecca. There is a checkpoint on the Jeddah side of the gate marking the boundaries of the sacred precinct beyond which non-Muslims are not permitted to travel.

FOLLOWING PAGES The prayer in the evening of Laylat al-Qadr. Pilgrims become of the most spiritualized in the last days of Ramadan, the month of fasting. The night of the 27th day of Ramadan is considered the holiest night of the year. This evening's prayer is to purify people of past sins and is joined by the second largest number of pilgrims next to the Hajj.

Mecca is the city of God, reflecting His absoluteness. To be here is to be at the center. To stand before the Ka'bah is to realize the journey's end. There is nowhere else to go here on earth for here is the goal of all terrestrial wayfaring. From Mindanao to Mauritania, Muslims keep the love of Mecca, this mother of cities, in their heart and yearn to come to its welcoming embrace, to stand before God's House in a city which was honored to be the birthplace and site of most of the life of God's friend, Habib Allah, the Prophet whose supreme triumph in life was to return to Mecca toward the end of his earthly journey victorious in being able to re-establish the religion of the One (*al-tawhid*) in a land which had long ago been witness to the cry of the father of monotheism, Abraham, to the One God. Mecca was never to forget the religion of Divine Unity again and remains to this day and, in fact, will remain to the end of time the spiritual center of the religion of Islam whose very *raison d'être* is to bear witness to the One who ultimately is the sole Reality that abides for "all things perish save the Face of God".

The building of the Ka'bah covered by a black cloth called the *kiswah*, adorned by verses from the Noble Qur'an embroidered in gold thread.

The Black Stone (*hajar al-aswad*), considered by Muslims to have descended from Heaven as the symbol of the covenant made between God and Adam and his progeny.

Some elderly people who have trouble walking make the *tawaf* on a palanquin carried by two men. When they come to the corner of the Black Stone, they hold up their hands in order to receive the *barakah* from the stone.

Pilgrims making the *tawaf*. The black cloth covering the Ka'bah is called the *kiswah*. Pilgrims chant the *talbiyah* during the *tawaf*.

ABOVE People holding on to the *kiswah* while praying.

OPPOSITE Footprints at the place where Abraham (Ibrahim) stood, called Maqam Ibrahim. The footprints are protected in a glass case to the east side of the Ka'bah.

ABOVE The Divine Name "Allah", the Supreme Name of God in Islam, adorns the center of this part of the band of the *kiswah*.

LEFT Using gold thread, workers embroider the Arabic script for "Allah", the name for God in Islam.

FOLLOWING PAGES Pilgrims conducting the sunset prayer (*maghrib*) completely fill the vast space around the Grand Mosque.

OPPOSITE Soldiers stand guard as the door is opened for washing inside the Ka'bah. Washing is done twice a year: on the first day of Rajab (the seventh month of the Islamic calendar) and during the first day of Dhu al-hijjah (the twelfth month). Inside the Ka'bah three golden clad pillars support the roof.

LEFT The governor of Mecca, on behalf of the king, is in charge of the washing of the Ka'bah. Diplomats and dignitaries take part in the ceremony. They come out afterwards holding the cloths that they used.

ABOVE Safa and Marwah are two stations in the vicinity of the Ka'bah between which pilgrims must walk quickly, almost at the pace of a run, or what is called *sa'y*. This is part of the ritual of the Hajj seen here photographed from the Safa side.

OPPOSITE Upon completion of the ritual of *sa'y*, pilgrims pray toward the Ka'bah from the hill of Safa. The rapid walk of *sa'y* represents symbolically the running to and fro of Hagar (Hajar), the wife of the Prophet Abraham (Ibrahim), in search of water for her son Ishmael (Ismail). Her search ended when the spring of Zamzam gushed forth miraculously.

OPPOSITE People are gathering for the *maghrib* prayers around the Grand Mosque. The minarets, which rise 93 meters, are lit up at dusk.

LEFT A fountain at the entrance of Mecca district. In the Noble Qur'an, water symbolizes Divine Mercy and in traditional Islamic cities water fountains are to be found nearly everywhere.

ABOVE The most popular merchandise sold in the shops around the Haram Mosque is the rosary (*subhah*). The Islamic rosary has ninety-nine beads corresponding to the ninety-nine "Beautiful Names of God" (*al-asma al-husna*).

OPPOSITE Although most of the older buildings of Mecca and Medina were destroyed as a result of the urban development of the past few years, some remain. Here is one with wooden lattice windows (*mashrabiyyah*) which have the effect of cooling the air inside the building.

ABOVE A view of Mount Hira where the Blessed Prophet received the first revelation. The photograph reveals many pilgrims climbing up the mountain despite signs saying "Do not climb," "Do not remove stones," etc.

OPPOSITE Underneath a rock painted white there is the small cave to which the Prophet would often come for meditation even before being chosen as Prophet and where he heard the first verses of the Qur'anic revelation. This site remains extremely holy in the eyes of Muslims.

Stages in the Hajj Pilgrimage

The stages of the rites of the Hajj (there being slight differences in various schools of Islamic law and views of jurists).
1. Pilgrims should arrive by the seventh day of the month of pilgrimage to the vicinity of Mecca where the men must purify themselves ritually and put on the *ihram* or dress of pilgrimage consisting of two pieces of white seamless cloth which is often used later for one's shroud. The women must also make the rites of purification but do not have to put on the *ihram* as do men. What is expected of them is to wear clean and simple clothing which is modest according to Islamic norms of female dress.

2. Upon arrival at the Great Mosque, the pilgrims must perform seven *tawaf* or circumambulations around the Ka'bah and then perform the *sa'y* between Safa and Marwah seven times. A special sermon is preached in the Great Mosque of Mecca.

3. In the morning of the eighth day, called *yawm al-tarwiyah* or "day of watering" because water is provided on this day for the next days, all pilgrims leave Mecca to an area outside the city called Mina where they spend the night. If, for some reason, this is impossible, the pilgrims may proceed directly from Mecca to Arafat on the ninth day.

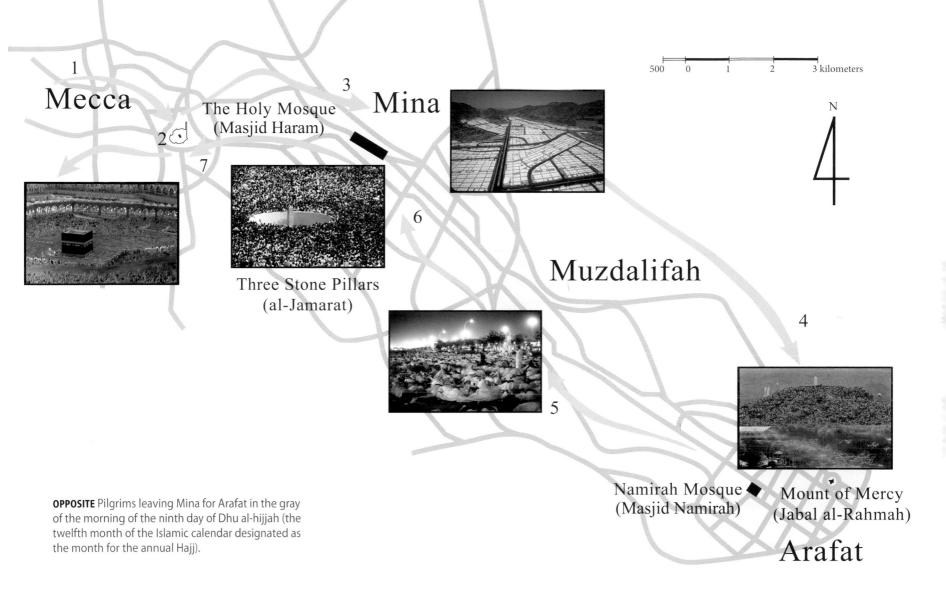

1 Mecca

The Holy Mosque
(Masjid Haram)

2

7

3 Mina

500 0 1 2 3 kilometers

N 4

6

Muzdalifah

Three Stone Pillars
(al-Jamarat)

5

4

Namirah Mosque
(Masjid Namirah)

Mount of Mercy
(Jabal al-Rahmah)

Arafat

OPPOSITE Pilgrims leaving Mina for Arafat in the gray of the morning of the ninth day of Dhu al-hijjah (the twelfth month of the Islamic calendar designated as the month for the annual Hajj).

4. In the morning of the ninth day, all pilgrims leave Mina for the plain of Arafat. Here, from noon to evening, the Noble Qur'an and prayers are recited (*wuquf*) and people try to climb Jabal al-Rahmah, the Mount of Mercy at the center of the plain of Arafat.

5. With sundown as the signal, pilgrims leave Arafat for Muzdalifah, which lies midway to Mina, and spend the night there. While there, they gather small pebbles (traditionally ten) to be used the next day at the rite of stone throwing.

6. After midnight or at dawn, pilgrims move to Mina and proceed to the largest stone pillar (called Jamarah of Aqabah) standing at the western edge of the three pillars located there. They then throw the stones they gathered earlier at the pillar symbolizing the Devil. The rite is done with consciousness that in throwing the stones at the pillar one is also casting away the evil in one's heart and soul. After this rite, an animal is usually sacrificed (hence the name of the celebration at the end of the pilgrimage as the *'id* of Sacrifice).

A group of Egyptian pilgrims arrive at the port of Jeddah.
Although most pilgrims arrive by plane nowadays,
chartered ships still ply the routes to Saudi Arabia from
Egypt, Sudan and Pakistan during the Hajj season.

LEFT During the Hajj, all available vehicles in Mecca are in use.

BELOW A group of pilgrims from Bangladesh at a standstill in congested traffic on the way to Arafat from Mina.

ABOVE A boy in *ihram*, the pilgrim's costume made of two pieces of white cotton cloth, following his parents during the Hajj.

RIGHT Mina, where some two million people throng during the Hajj. Tents are allocated to pilgrims in groups according to their country of origin, the arrangements being made by a special agency called the Mutawalla, which is in charge of all travel arrangements for the pilgrims.

Pilgrims of Indian origin from South Africa performing the *maghrib* prayers at Mina. In contrast to what one observes in Arab countries, the women are standing not behind but adjacent to the men.

The national flag of Saudi Arabia, bearing the Islamic testimony of faith "There is no god but Allah and Muhammad is his Messenger," flies from an escort car of the group of pilgrims who are guests of the governor of Mecca.

ABOVE Tents in Mina on the ninth day of the month of pilgrimage. A city of semi-permanent tents, fully air-conditioned and made of fireproof materials, have replaced those destroyed by fire in 1997. On this day, Mina is deserted while everyone visits Arafat.

LEFT The Grand Mosque on the Day of Arafat, the ninth day of the month of pilgrimage, in 2000. With two million pilgrims in Arafat on this day, the *kiswah*, the black cloth covering the Ka'bah, is being changed in the empty mosque.

Men have some of their hair cut off and the *ihram* is removed. Pilgrims stay there for two more days, on the tenth and eleventh, during which stones are thrown at the two smaller pillars, also representing the Devil, and then return to Mecca where the final circumambulation of parting (*tawaf al-ifadah*) is performed. Most jurists have given the view that the *tawaf* at the Ka'bah should be done on the tenth day.

7. All pilgrims leave Mina by the twelfth day and return to Mecca where those who had not completed the final *tawaf* do so. Then begins the great celebration of Id al-adha, the Feast of Sacrifice, and the pilgrims gain the honorific titles of *hajji* for men and *hajjiyah* for women.

Pilgrims on the Mount of Mercy (Rahman) at Arafat on the ninth day of the month of pilgrimage and the climax of the rites. Here they perform *wuquf*, which consists of the recitation of the Noble Qur'an and intense prayer with all their heart. Water sprinklers function all day to relieve the excruciating heat.

Pilgrims performing *wuquf* at Arafat. During the rites of pilgrimage, people recite continuously the *talbiyah*, which is a prayer in praise of God starting with "labbayka, allahumma labbayk" (At Thy Service, O Lord, at Thy Service).

Pilgrims performing *wuquf* at the Mount of Mercy. Nothing is allowed to be worn besides the *ihram*, but one is permitted to carry a parasol to ward off the sun.

The climax of the Day of Arafat. Two million pilgrims attend the noon prayer (*dhuhr*), which is shortened and combined with the afternoon prayer (*asr*). This is followed by a sermon reminding the pilgrims of the Day of Judgement.

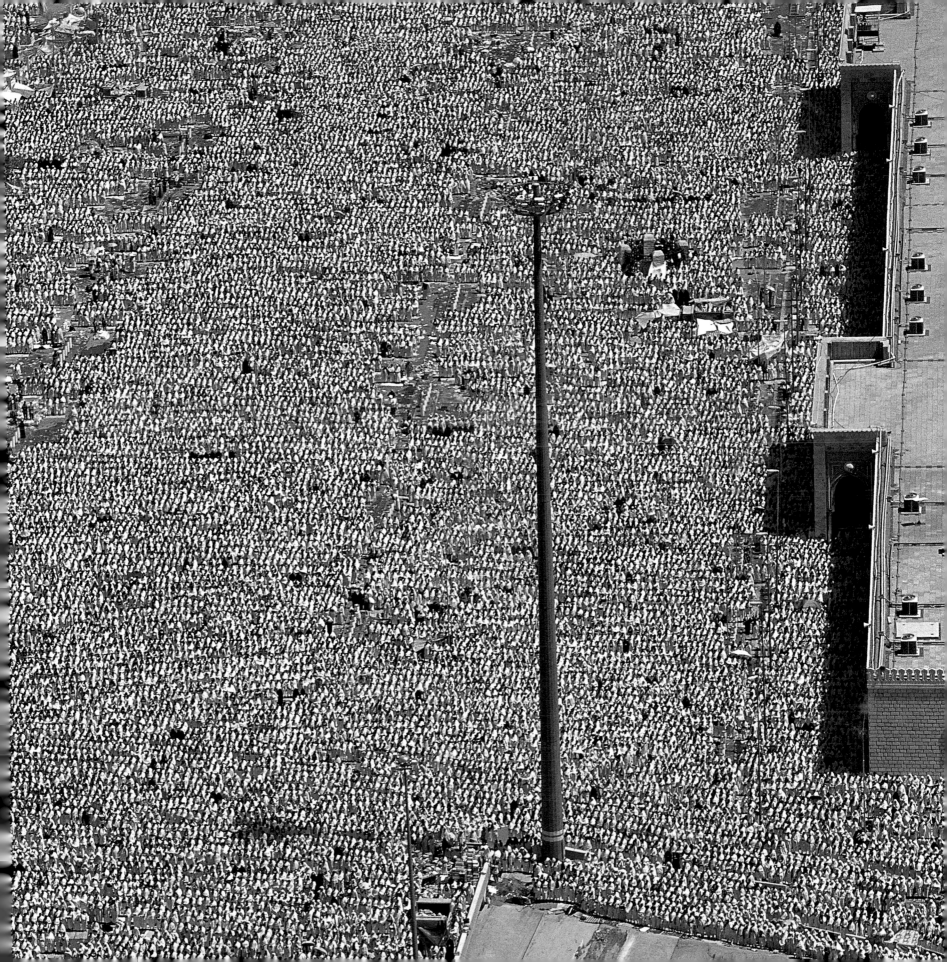

ABOVE A vast crowd leaving Arafat at the moment of sunset. At this time everyone, whether walking or in cars, prays audibly and the deep sound of the prayers reverberates throughout the vast plains of Arafat. The building in the background is the Namirah Mosque.

OPPOSITE Pilgrims performing the *wuquf* are filled with emotion. Many shed tears before they leave Arafat.

ABOVE Pilgrims arriving from Arafat to Muzdalifah must spend their time here after midnight. Therefore, the wasteland of Muzdalifah becomes so crowded that there is hardly space to put one's foot. Here, most pilgrims gather the stones which they will cast later in Mina.

OPPOSITE A vast crowd leaving Arafat for Muzdalifah at the moment of sunset. There are eight motorways and two pedestrian roads between Arafat and Muzdalifah, along which the two million pilgrims make their way.

FOLLOWING PAGES On the tenth day, the pilgrims who have returned to Mina gather for the rite of the casting of stones at the pillars symbolizing the Devil. The area around the pillars is extremely crowded and dangerous for women, children and the elderly, who may therefore ask one of the men accompanying them to perform the rite for them. On this day, stone is cast only at the largest of the pillars.

The rite of the casting of stones at the two smaller
pillars, which like the larger one symbolize the
forces of evil, takes place. The pillars are called
Jamarat in Arabic.

It is traditional for people to cut off hair after the rite of the casting of stones. Women and some men cut only a lock or two of their hair while other men shave their heads completely, as seen here.

The end of the Hajj is marked by the sacrifice of an animal in celebration of the sacrifice of the prophet Abraham (Ibrahim). Here, a herd of camels is being brought for sacrifice. The celebration at the end of the pilgrimage is called Id al-adha and it lasts four days, during which those who have made the Hajj before often also perform the sacrifice of an animal in their home town, the meat then being given to the poor.

ABOVE AND RIGHT Pilgrims used to slaughter animals for the sacrifice themselves, but now it is mostly carried out in the slaughter houses in Muzdalifah with the exception of a few pilgrims who do it themselves. The meat is distributed to the pilgrims. This photograph shows the evening meal on the eighth day of the month of pilgrimage.

A group of pilgrims from Indonesia reciting prayers after
the rite of casting of stones. All women, even those who
hide their faces behind a veil in their own country,
perform the pilgrimage with their faces revealed and
only their hair covered.

Men and women both wear their best clothing for the
Id al-adha, the women usually dressing in black or white.
But there is much diversity in traditional Islamic dress, as
the colorful habit of this group of African women reveals.

ABOVE A security and crowd control room in Mina. Over 500 surveillance cameras are set up on the pilgrimage route from Mecca to Arafat.

OPPOSITE Those who pitch tents on hilltops or surroundings are usually foreign workers in Saudi Arabia who often make the pilgrimage individually. There are some five million such workers and many among them perform the annual pilgrimage every year.

LEFT Evening (*maghrib*) prayers at the camping area in Mina. Most pilgrims leave this area and return to Mecca on the twelfth day but they do spend at least one night at Mina. This and other steps in the Hajj follow the precedent established by the wonts (*sunnah*) of the Blessed Prophet who made the pilgrimage in 10/632.

FOLLOWING PAGES After the completion of the rites at Mina, pilgrims return to Mecca for the farewell *tawaf* or circumambulation (*tawaf al-wida*) at the Haram or Grand Mosque. Those who cannot enter the holy precinct, perform the *tawaf* on the second floor of the mosque, in the basement or even outside the immense complex of the mosque.

Medina the Radiant

It was in this miraculous oasis—gentle, hospitable and full of bounties—that the last years of the life of the Blessed Prophet were spent, where the first Islamic community was established, where the Prophet died, and where many of his companions and closest members of his family are buried. The earth of Medina is blessed by the fact that it contains the body of God's last chosen prophet, a blessedness that one feels while walking on its hallowed ground. No wonder that in days of old many a pious man would dismount from his horse a long way outside of the city and would walk the rest of the way in order to be respectful of the land that contains in its bosom the earthly remains of such a precious being. Even a generation ago, Medina was like a vast garden, with majestic palm trees surrounding the houses and markets of the city, giving an impression of plentitude and bounty. One might, in fact, say that whereas Mecca represents the reality of the Divine as the Absolute, Medina reflects His reality as the Infinite. There is a feminine quality to the city in the sense that it is not harsh but gentle. Even its people display the trait of gentleness, reflecting the character of the Prophet about whom the Noble Qur'an has said: "O thou art of a tremendous Character."

Evening prayers at the Mosque of the Prophet (Masjid al-Nabi), 1996. During the twenty days preceding and following the annual Hajj, nearly all of the two million pilgrims visit Medina as well but they are not all there at the same time, as is the case with Mecca.

ABOVE Pilgrims heading for the evening (*maghrib*) prayers through the marble-floored complex of the Mosque of the Prophet. Usually the *maghrib* prayers are the most crowded.

OPPOSITE A view of a section of the inside of the Mosque of the Prophet, part of the extension completed in 1995. The new parts of the mosque have elaborate air-conditioning and a cooling water system to compensate for the extreme heat, especially during the summer season.

After all, this is the abode of the Prophet dominated by his mausoleum and mosque. His *barakah* is felt throughout the confines of the town. The heart yearns to visit Medina precisely because this is the city of the Prophet, its mosque the model of all mosques, its traditions the source of so many Islamic practices. To love God one must love His Prophet. To love Mecca also requires loving Medina. The two cities, in fact, form a single sacred reality for the vast majority of Muslims who live outside their vicinity, a reality at once blessed and luminous. Yes, there is indeed something of the Muhammadan Light, the light associated with the inner reality of the Blessed Prophet that still emanates in his city and bestows upon Medina a special *barakah*, a sweet presence which is associated with the being whom it welcomed to its fold, the being who is interred in its earth and who made Medina the capital of a vast new order.

Although that political order no longer exists as a unity, this first capital of the Islamic world continues to be loved by all Muslims near and far. Today, as in days of old, all the faithful pray for the opportunity to be able to experience the Muhammadan *barakah* which is still so palpable within the confines of this "illuminated city", still the capital of the Blessed Prophet's dominion.

The Friday congregational prayer at the Mosque of the Prophet is always attended by the people of Medina as well as pilgrims. That is why the space holding 190,000 worshippers invariably becomes full and many listen to the sermon (*khutbah*), which forms part of the Friday prayers, outside under the heat of the sun.

ماكان محمد أبا أحد من رجالكم ولكن رسول الله وخاتم النبيين

This photograph, taken with special permission at midnight when the Mosque of the Prophet was closed, shows the southern wall of the room (known as the "Blessed Room" by Muslims) in which the Prophet is buried with Abu Bakr and Umar, the first two caliphs, beside him.

116

ABOVE The Mosque of the Prophet adjacent to the Prophet's tomb is, along with the Ka'bah, the most sacred place for Muslims.

OPPOSITE The *mihrab* or prayer niche built in the direction of Mecca before which the Blessed Prophet himself prayed. This mosque was built by the Prophet adjacent to his dwelling when he first migrated from Mecca to Medina.

Pilgrims offering prayers next to the tomb known as the
Blessed Prophet's meeting room. Pilgrims are forbidden
to enter the chamber containing the Prophet's tomb and
it is therefore here that they feel closest to him. It is here
that their hearts are most uplifted, with most pilgrims
praying intensely with tears in their eyes.

The Wahhabi, who dominate religious life in Saudi Arabia, oppose visitation of the tombs of saints, but offering prayers at the tomb of the Blessed Prophet is permitted. The love of the Blessed Prophet is central in Islam.

ABOVE A young Pakistani boy, son of a laborer in Medina, praying with the use of his rosary (*subhah*) while awaiting the time of the canonical prayers (*salat*).

RIGHT A pilgrim from West Africa reciting the Qur'an in the vast space of the Mosque of the Prophet outside the period of the Hajj. The short pilgrimage (*al-umrah*) can be and is performed by numerous people throughout the year so that the wave of pilgrims to Mecca and Medina never ceases.

ABOVE The extension of the Mosque of the Prophet in Medina, which was completed in 1995, has provided seating capacity for some 260,000 for prayers. With the outside space all covered with marble, there is enough room for a million people to pray at the mosque, making it the second largest mosque in the world after the Grand Mosque of Mecca.

OPPOSITE The tomb of the Blessed Prophet Muhammad—may peace and blessings be upon him—in Medina. The green-colored dome and the Ka'bah are the two most recognizable symbols of the religion of Islam.

ABOVE People coming out of the Mosque of the Prophet after the *maghrib* prayers when all the shops around the mosque open their doors again and the area becomes very lively. As for restaurants, they begin to serve food after the *isha* prayer.

OPPOSITE Two female pilgrims walk at dusk in the enclosure of the Mosque of the Prophet, where the floor is lavishly decorated with an arabesque pattern.

An aerial view of al-Baqi cemetery, the oldest and historically the most significant cemetery in Medina.

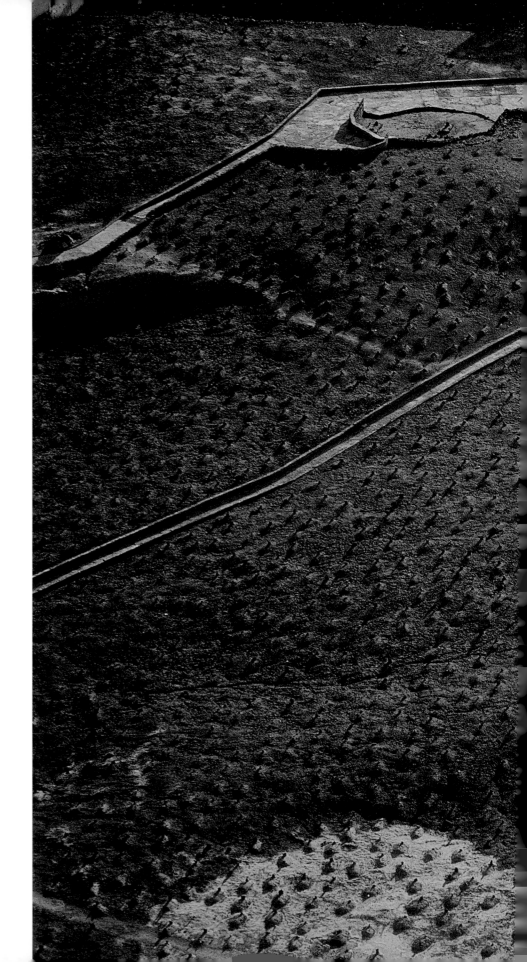

During the holy month of Ramadan, the most sacred month of the Islamic calendar, all adult Muslims who have the physical capability are obliged to fast from dawn to sunset. Here, pilgrims are offered food to break their fast at the Mosque of the Prophet.

Saudi children help in the preparation of the meal to break the fast (*iftar*). Wealthier Muslims by tradition prepare food for the needy at this time. Here, during every evening of Ramadan, wealthy Saudi families provide *iftar* for whoever requests it.

ABOVE LEFT People being offered *iftar* in Medina. Other than pilgrims, laborers often participate in these free meals. Feeding the poor is a religious obligation in Islam.

ABOVE RIGHT A woman pilgrim from Indonesia has wandered into an area designated for men and is awaiting the time to break the fast. In the early days of Islam, *iftar* consisted usually of dates, bread and water but now a variety of dishes are prepared for the occasion.

FOLLOWING PAGES Over a hundred thousand people are having *iftar* in the vast garden surrounding the Mosque of the Prophet. Before breaking their fast, people offer a prayer of thanksgiving to God for having been able to fast during the day.

The early prayers on the morning after the end of Ramadan marking the Id al-fitr, which is the great Muslim holiday. On this occasion, over a million people consisting of pilgrims as well as the people of Medina come to the Mosque of the Prophet, the worshippers overflowing to the spaces around the mosque.

A total of 250 umbrellas shade the huge enclosure surrounding the Mosque of the Prophet. Designed to protect pilgrims at prayer from the fierce Arabian sun, the umbrellas are opened in two stages from five o'clock in the morning and closed around sunset.

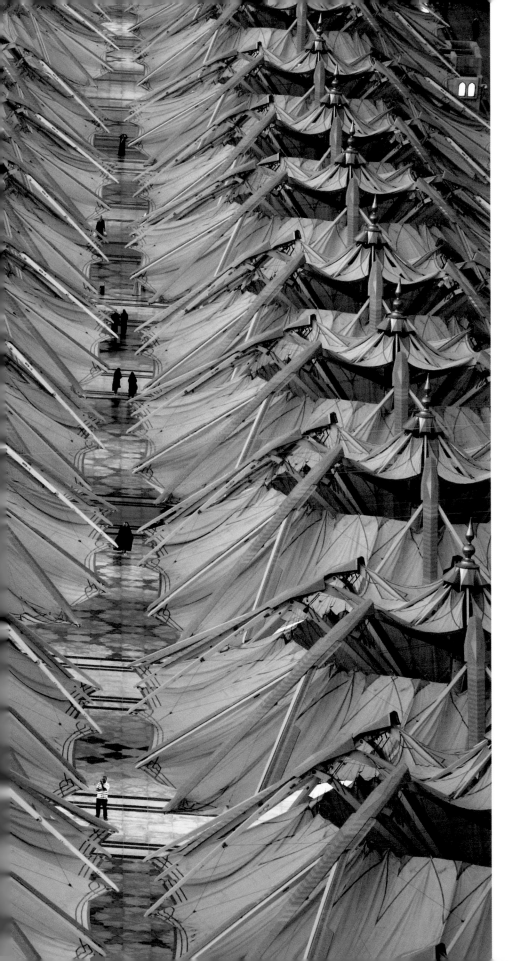

Made of non-flammable material to protect pilgrims in case of fire, the square umbrellas are massive, measuring 25.5 x 25.5 meters. It takes approximately three minutes for them to unfold, which is done with an electric system. Installation began in 2008 and took three years.

ABOVE All the umbrellas closed down tightly for the night, pilgrims gather in the enclosure of the Mosque of the Prophet for the *isha* prayers.

OPPOSITE Early in the morning, the umbrellas begin to open in unison. The opening of the umbrellas starts with no warning or sound, and pilgrims who have encountered the huge devices look up, overwhelmed.

The Quba Mosque where the Blessed Prophet first prayed when he entered Medina. He gathered stones with his own hands and with the help of his followers built a simple edifice, which is considered to be the first mosque in the world.

The *mihrab* of the Qiblatayn Mosque (literally meaning having two *qiblah* or directions of prayer). During the first years of the advent of Islam, the *qiblah* was in the direction of Jerusalem and then by Divine Command the direction was changed toward Mecca. The original version of this mosque was used during that transitional period and therefore had two *qiblah*. The current edifice was constructed recently at the side of the earlier mosque.

ABOVE Thai pilgrims selling merchandise from their homeland. During the pilgrimage, people are allowed to buy and sell goods which often provides for the expense of their journey. This tradition goes back to the earliest days of Islam.

RIGHT Jewelers in the bazaar around the Mosque of the Prophet. Many women purchase jewelry during the pilgrimage and jewelry shops have the largest number of customers during the months of the Hajj and Ramadan.

Pilgrims from Daghestan, a Muslim land in present-day Russia. They had made the journey of 5,800 kilometers in eight days through Iran, Iraq and Jordan.

A poor family of pilgrims from Pakistan who were camping on vacant land adjacent to the Mosque of the Prophet for a week.

A group of Turkish pilgrims at the foot of Mount Uhud, the site in northern Medina of the famous and intense battle in Islamic history during which the idolatrous Quraysh tribe from Mecca defeated the Islamic army. During this battle, the Blessed Prophet was injured but the Meccans did not pursue the Muslims and returned to their own city.

Pilgrims praying at the tomb of the Blessed Prophet's uncle, Hamzah, who died at the battle of Uhud along with seventy other martyrs. In this battle, which took place on 23 March AD 625, the Islamic army, consisting of a thousand men, faced an army three times in size led by the Quraysh from Mecca.

149

ABOVE A group of Turkish pilgrims praying and mourning at the battlefield of Uhud.

RIGHT A group of Chinese Muslims from Kashgar/Kashi visiting, like almost all other pilgrims, the battlefield of Uhud.

ABOVE A group of Nigerian pilgrims at Uhud.

RIGHT A group of Pakistani pilgrims praying on a hilltop at Uhud.

The Miqat Mosque. Located in the Al-Aqiq valley, nine kilometers south of the Mosque of the Prophet, pilgrims bound for Mecca change here into the pilgrim's *ihram*. This custom is said to have come about because on his way to Mecca the Blessed Prophet Muhammad changed into his *ihram* under a tree that grew here.

ABOVE Pilgrims donning the *ihram* at the Miqat Mosque to go to Mecca for pilgrimage. Before putting on the *ihram*, they perform the ritual washing of their bodies (*ghusl*).

OPPOSITE While wearing the *ihram*, a Muslim is forbidden from hunting, killing, arguing, violence, deceit and sexual activity.

The *ihram*, consisting of two pieces of seamless white cloth, is worn on the naked body and symbolizes the state of man in his primordial condition.

The *ihram*, especially of one's first pilgrimage, is washed in Zamzam water and then put away to be used as one's shroud. To wear the *ihram* itself symbolizes having died to the profane world.

When wearing the *ihram*, one must remove all adornments. In fact, all signs of position and status in society are removed and all men face God with their soul laid bare and independent of all worldly distinctions.

Children of foreign laborers and residents at one of the many Qur'anic schools in Medina. The children are from many nationalities, reflecting the different national backgrounds of the laborers and the many pilgrims who have come from all over the world to Medina and then have decided to remain there.

The King Fahd Complex for the Printing of the Holy Qur'an in Medina is the largest Qur'anic printing facility in the world, printing 10 million copies per year. Established in 1985, it prints in 39 languages. By 2007, it had printed 128 million copies. Missprints or missing pages are not permissible in the Holy Qur'an, so the inspection system is strict, requiring multiple stations.

A historic picture of the train leaving Medina in 1908 when the railway was called the Hijaz Railway. Some of the track between Damascus and Medina is to be found to this day.

The Ottomans built a railway to link Damascus to Medina. The line was opened in 1908 and trains remained in service until 1924 when Medina fell to the forces of the Saudis. This steam engine remains in the station of the historic railway.

The opening ceremony of the Hijaz Railway in Medina in 1908. There were plans to extend the railway to Mecca, but they were never realized.

Pilgrims and the people of Medina fill the enclosure of the Mosque of the Prophet for Friday congregational prayer. The supporting pillar of each umbrella is equipped with a misting fan, so even in summer when the outside temperature reaches 45° Celsius it is close to four degrees cooler under the umbrella, providing a space for pleasant prayer.

The Arabian Peninsula

A bridge between three continents, a neighbor to the
African and Persian worlds as well as the eastern Mediterranean region, this stark land of great beauty and purity
was witness to many prophets and the scene of many
episodes of the sacred history of the Abrahamic world.
But it remained outside of the arena of world history until
it was visited by the archangel Gabriel who, on the order
of God, brought the Qur'anic revelation and revealed the
last total message of Heaven to one of the sons of Arabia,
the Blessed Prophet of Islam. Henceforth, the land of
Arabia became inseparable from the life of the Prophet.
In the same way that the aroma of the frankincense of this
land reached the Roman Empire and medieval Europe, the
spiritual fragrance of Arabia, holy to Islam, is sensed by
Muslims near and far. Who among the Muslim faithful ever
comes to Arabia without becoming deeply imbued with
the sacred quality of the land chosen by God for His final
revelation?

The ruins of Mada'in Salih, part of a complex of ruins in the desert in
the northwestern region of the Arabian peninsula, most of them being
tombs of Nabateans who formed a civilization in that region in the early
centuries of the Christian era. The center of their civilization was in and
around Petra in present-day Jordan.

The very starkness of the landscape of Arabia opens the soul bare and naked before God, and the intensity of the sun reminds man of the majesty of the One before whom all multiplicity dissolves in the same way that in the glow of the sun of the Arabian desert the "many" seem to disappear while the ubiquitous presence of light symbolizing the Presence of the One remains. And then there are the lush green oases growing as if out of nowhere in the middle of the arid desert, oases profuse with life reminding man of the Divine Mercy which, according to a sacred saying (*hadith qudsi*), precedes God's wrath. The central lands of Arabia, and especially the Hijaz, have been blessed by God with the seal of holiness, and this land with its vast deserts symbolizing infinity and majestic peaks reflecting the quality of absoluteness and transcendence, will remain to the end of time, and despite all that men may do to defile it, a land reverberating with the presence of the Sacred.

These graves have stylized decorations on flat surfaces cut from a giant sandstone wall. The graves belonged not to an individual but to a whole family and funeral rites were performed there each time a family member died.

LEFT TOP There are many small alcoves such as these in the inside wall. In ancient times, when it was customary to rebury the dead, cinerary urns of various families were consigned to such shelves.

LEFT BOTTOM The remains of a temple destroyed by weather. The Nabatean people controlled this land around 200 to 300 AD, but in 106 AD the Nabatean were conquered by Rome and perished.

OPPOSITE An epitaph on a grave inscribed in the Nabatean language on the white section above the statue at the center of this photograph. A white plastic board has been placed there to prevent erosion of the inscription. The Nabatean alphabet is considered the forerunner of the Arabic alphabet.

ABOVE Prehistoric drawings carved on a rock in Jubbah, an oasis in the Nafud desert which lies 100 kilometers north of Ha'il. Countless drawings from the prehistoric era to the Bedouin time of camel herding are to be found in the area.

LEFT Prehistoric engravings on a cave wall in the desert area near Ha'il in the middle of the Arabian peninsula.

175

An oasis in al-Ula near Mada'in Salih where one finds water veins which have made possible the date palm grove. This area was a transit point of the old caravan route stretching from the Yemen to Palestine.

The traditional Arab sport of camel racing continues to this day. Here, one can see the famous race for the King's Cup held outside the capital of Saudi Arabia, Riyadh. Some four hundred camels usually participate and the race takes about half an hour. In the 1970s and 1980s, around three thousand camels would participate and dazzling sums were awarded to the winners.

This is a traditional dish called Quzī, consisting of baby camel roasted whole, surrounded by rice. Here, villagers participate in the feast given by the governor after the camel race.

ABOVE Baby camels being transported to the meat market. The modernization of the past few decades in Saudi Arabia has decreased greatly the demand for camels as a means of transportation.

OPPOSITE A boy of the nomadic Tohma al-Qahtani tribe living in a mountain district in southwest Saudi Arabia on the border with Yemen. Men wear fragrant wild flowers in their hair.

ABOVE AND RIGHT A Bedouin family living in a traditional woolen tent. Like many other Bedouins, this family has lived here for many years and even has some modern facilities in the tent, such as a washing machine run by a generator.

LEFT A village elder relaxing in his tent. Although many Bedouins have now taken up agriculture, love of the freedom of the desert still runs strongly in their veins.

OPPOSITE Although most Bedouins in Arabia have become settled in urban centers in recent decades, some still remain nomads as seen here where a Bedouin woman is holding her child in a traditional Bedouin tent.

RIGHT Although the living space of this girl inside her Bedouin tent has not changed for millennia, she is watching television, bringing a completely alien world to the ambience in that traditional space.

Interior of a house in the Asir region. Three or four
stories high, it has a spiral staircase in the center.
There is a guest room for men on the second floor.

A house in Dhahran al-Janub, an oasis in the mountainous Asir province. Built by piling up rammed earth, its structure would have provided good protection in times of battle in the past.

Although mostly a desert, Saudi Arabia has vast natural underground water that has been used in recent years for agriculture.

Glossary

Adhan The Muslim call to prayers recited five times a day throughout the Islamic world.

Ahl al-bayt The "household of the Prophet", held in great reverence by all orthodox Muslims, especially the Shi'ites.

Arkan Literally "pillars", it refers to the four cardinal directions as well as the four corners of the Ka'bah.

Azal Pre-eternity, referring to that "moment" before all time in which man made his primordial covenant (al-mithaq) with God.

Barakah The grace which issues from God and runs through the arteries of the universe.

Bayt al-atiq The "Ancient House", another name used by Muslims for the Ka'bah.

Dhu al-hijjah The twelfth month of the lunar Islamic calendar during which the Hajj takes place.

Din al-fitrah The primordial religion or the religion that is inherent to man's primordial nature.

Du'a Individual prayer which a Muslim can and should perform often. In contrast to the canonical prayers whose language must always be Arabic, the individual prayers may be said in whatever language is convenient for the believer.

Ghayb The invisible and, by extension, the spiritual world.

Ghazz Literally "battle" but used most often in reference to the early battles of the nascent Islamic community against the Meccans and their allies before the latter accepted Islam.

Ghusl Total ritual ablution of the body.

Hadith A saying of the Prophet of Islam. These sayings were compiled by later scholars into canonical collections.

Hajar al-aswad The Black Stone at a corner of the Ka'bah symbolizing man's original covenant with God.

Hajj The annual pilgrimage to Mecca.

Hajj al-umrah The shorter pilgrimage which can be performed at any time during the year, its conditions being simpler than the annual Hajj and limited to the Ka'bah and its adjacent area.

Hajji The title given to a male who has performed the annual Hajj.

Hajjiyah The title given to a female who has performed the annual Hajj.

Hanif (hunafa) A follower of primordial monotheism.

Haram Holy or sacred precinct and, more specifically, the holy precinct of Mecca.

Hubal The most prominent idol kept at the Ka'bah by pre-Islamic Arabs during the "Age of Ignorance" (jahiliyyah).

Id al-adha The Feast of Sacrifice which comes at the end of the rites of the Hajj.

Id al-qurban Persian for the Feast of Sacrifice, a term that is used also in many other Islamic languages.

Iftar The meal with which the fast during the month of Ramadan is broken at the time of sunset.

Ihram Two pieces of unsewn white cloth worn by men who are to make the Hajj.

Isha The name of the night prayers performed after the maghrib which must be performed before midnight.

Jahiliyyah Literally the "Age of Ignorance", the term used by Muslims to refer to the historical period in Arabia before the advent of the Islamic revelation.

Jamarah of Aqabah The largest pillar in Mina symbolizing Satan, against which stones (pebbles) are cast.

Jiddah Maternal ancestor, the title of Eve in whose honor the city of Jeddah is named.

Jihad Literally exertion in the path of God, it has been often mistranslated in English as holy war.

Jihad al-akbar The great jihad, referring to the inner battle against the lower and passionate tendencies of the soul.

Jihad al-asghar The lesser jihad or the outer battle to preserve Islam and defend its borders.

Ka'bah The "House of God", the cubic structure in Mecca built by Abraham and, according to Islamic belief, going back to Adam who built the first temple at the present site as the earthly reflection of the Divine Temple in Heaven.

Khandaq The "Ditch", used in reference to one of the famous early battles in which the Muslims of Medina dug a ditch around the city to protect themselves from the attacks of the Meccans.

Kiswah The black cloth with golden verses of the Qur'an which covers the Ka'bah.

Khutbah The sermon delivered on Fridays during the congregational prayers.

Laylat al-Qadr The "Night of Power", usually celebrated on the night of the 27th of Ramadan when the Qur'an first descended through the Archangel Gabriel upon the soul of the Prophet.

Madinat al-munawwarah Medina the Radiant, the traditional Islamic name for the city of Medina.

Madinat al-nabi Literally the "City of the Prophet", which came to replace the older name of Yathrib that henceforth came to be known simply as Medina.

Maghrib Meaning both the west and the setting of the sun, it also designates the time of the evening prayers performed after sunset.

Mahshar Place of the Resurrection which, according to Islamic eschatology, will take place bodily at the Day of Judgement.

Makkat al-mukarramah Mecca the Blessed, the traditional Islamic name for the city of Mecca.

Masjid al-nabi The Mosque of the Prophet in Medina which is the prototype of all later mosques.

Mihrab The niche in the wall of the mosque indicating the direction of the qiblah before which the leader of the prayers (imam) and the worshippers stand during the canonical daily prayers.

Miraj The nocturnal ascent of the Prophet of Islam from Jerusalem to the Divine Presence.

Mithaq The covenant made between God and Adam and all his progeny before the creation of the world.

Muhajirun Those who migrated with the Prophet from Mecca to Medina in AD 622.

Mujahid One who carries out jihad either intellectually and spiritually or externally and physically, or both.

Qiblah The direction of the daily prayers toward Mecca (the Ka'bah).

Qiblah al-ula The first qiblah, that is, Jerusalem, toward which Muslims prayed before they were ordered by God to pray toward Mecca or, more exactly, the Ka'bah.

Ramadan The ninth month of the lunar Islamic calendar, the holiest month of the year, during which Muslims fast from dawn to sunset and when the Qur'anic revelation began.

Sakinah The Divine Peace which descends upon the believers by God's command.

Salah/Salat The canonical prayers performed five times a day.

Sa'y Rapid movement between walking and running which pilgrims perform seven times between Safa and Marwah in emulation of Hajar/Hagar's running to and fro to find water for her son Ismail/Ishmael.

Shahadah Both the testimony of Islamic faith and the visible world.

Shari'ah The Divine Law of Islam based upon the two basic sources, the Qur'an and the sunnah.

Shaytan Satan or the Devil.

Shaytan al-rajim The accursed Satan or, literally, Satan against whom stone is cast.

Sunnah The wonts or actions of the Blessed Prophet which are the object of emulation by Muslims.

Talbiyah The prayer in praise of God (at Thy service, O Lord, at Thy service) repeated throughout the rites of the Hajj, especially during circumambulation around the Ka'bah.

Tawaf Circumambulation around the Ka'bah.

Tawaf al-wida The final circumambulation around the Ka'bah at the end of the Hajj.

Tawhid The principle of unity and integration, which is the central doctrine of Islam.

Ummah The religious community following a prophet, such as Jews and Christians, but used most often in reference to the Islamic community in its totality.

Wuquf Prayers offered in Arafat from the noon to the evening on the ninth day of the Hajj, marking one of the central events of the rites of pilgrimage.

Yawm al-tarwiyah Literally the "day of watering", it refers to the eighth day of the Hajj when water is provided for the rest of the period of the pilgrimage.

Zamzam The sacred spring in Mecca near the Ka'bah discovered with the help of an angel by Hajar/Hagar when she was looking for water for her son Ismail/Ishmael.